With love,
Kim
xxo

HILL SPIRITS III

An Anthology by Writers of Northumberland County

Edited by

Felicity Sidnell Reid

Gwynn Scheltema

Susan Statham

blue denim press

Copyright © 2017: Copyright for the anthology as a body of work shall remain with the Northumberland Arts Association Inc., and with the individual Contributors for their respective contributions.
Published by Blue Denim Press Inc.
Cover design: Joanne Kasunic
Original Cover Art: Susan Statham
Published in Canada
ALL RIGHTS RESERVED: No part of this publication may be reproduced, stored in a retrieval system or transmitted in any form or by any means without the prior written permission of the publisher and the authors, except in the case of a reviewer, who may quote brief passages in a review.
DISCLAIMER: The views and opinions expressed in this anthology are those of the authors and do not necessarily reflect the official policy or position of the publisher, the editors, the Spirit of the Hills Writers Group, or the Northumberland Arts Association Inc.

Canadian Cataloguing in Publication Data
Hill Spirits : an anthology by writers of Northumberland County. -- First edition.

Volume III edited by Felicity Sidnell Reid, Gwynn Scheltema, Susan Statham.
Issued in print and electronic formats.
ISBN 978-1-927882-28-3 (v. 3 : softcover).--ISBN 978-1-927882-29-0 (v. 3 : Kindle).--ISBN 978-1-927882-30-6 (v. 3 : EPUB)

1. Canadian literature (English)--Ontario--Northumberland. 2. Canadian literature (English)--21st century. I. Sidnell Reid, Felicity, 1936-, editor II. Scheltema, Gwynn, 1954-, editor III. Statham, Susan, 1951-, editor

PS8255.O5H55 2012 C810.8'0971357 C2012-905381-3
C2012-905382-1

"A story is not like a road to follow…it's more like a house. You go inside and stay there for a while, wandering back and forth and settling where you like and discovering how the room and corridors relate to each other, how the world outside is altered by being viewed from these windows."

Alice Munro

WELCOME

Northumberland Spirit of the Hills Writers Group, like many Canadians across this land, are celebrating Canada in 2017 and honouring our ancestors, whether they are new to Canada or were here long before Canada existed.

The editors' first objective has been to preserve the writers' voices, including the creative coinage allowable to writers. Many of these pieces celebrate the land itself and the way we choose to enjoy it. From histories to light-hearted fiction, from personal memoir and poetry to non-fiction essays, you'll find a great variety of writing and many different perspectives on this great land.

The editors also gratefully acknowledge the meticulous copy-editing of this book by Marie-Lynn Hammond and thank her on behalf of all the contributors.

We hope you enjoy our collection, which says, "Here's to you, Canada!"

Felicity Sidnell Reid
Gwynn Scheltema
Susan Statham

Table of Contents

Rene Schmidt

THE CANOE TRIP

You wake before dawn. You bring only a thermos of fresh-brewed coffee because all else is packed. The car and the canoe on the roof are speckled with dew. Everything is ready. You drive north on deserted roads, leaving the thick city smells behind. The air gets cleaner, cooler. The coffee in your travel mug is better than on commuting days. When you stop for gas you pull on the straps holding the canoe. It doesn't budge and you smile. Perfect. Your clothes are old and warm and comfortable and you have dressed in layers. The outer layer, a fisherman's vest, has lots of pockets for a pocket knife, matches, canoe route map, duct tape, and some repair wire. Wallet and watch are already safe in the zippered pocket.

You arrive as the park office opens for the morning. There are few cars at the parking lot.

"Any bottles or cans?" she asks.

"No."

"Good."

Your few supplies are in plastic bags and reusable containers. You show her on the map where you will be going. "Any bears?"

"Not lately," she replies.

You untie the canoe and carefully lift one side up and slide it toward you. The Styrofoam blocks make strange squealing noises as you slide the vessel outward and then lift it onto your shoulders. As you lower it to the water, ripples spread silently outward on the glass flat surface.

A kingfisher darts from tree to tree. Mist rises farther out, little vapour persons appearing and circling and vanishing again, revealing warmer water out there. You arrange your packs carefully and load in an extra paddle and an extra lifejacket. J-stroke, straight stroke, J-stroke, straight stroke: a pattern develops and the rhythm sets in. With conscious effort the paddle does not touch the gunnels or make any extra sound.

Silently gliding through the water you disturb nothing, yet see all. You pass a loon, who alternates between watching you warily and peering underwater like a child peeking under blankets. Suddenly he is off, slipping roundly beneath the water after an unseen fish. The sun slowly warms the lake surface. Ripples form and sparkle like fields of new-cut diamonds out on the lake ahead of you.

You skirt the shoreline to avoid a growing breeze. Here and there are campsites neatly hidden along the shoreline. At one, a red canoe is drawn up and a flicker of light reveals a morning campfire. Voices speak softly, unaware of you, and seconds later you pass the thin olfactory vapour of a clean cedar fire.

You paddle on. Around a point you head into the lake and the wind brings up ripples. Now and then a small whitecap forms and disappears. You choose an angle that lets you hold your course as you paddle with long straight strokes. Ripples tap the canoe's bow. Your arms begin to tire but you cannot switch sides because of the breeze.

Is that the portage?

No, not yet. Farther down the little bay. Is that it?

There is a tiny yellow dot on a tree. The map verifies your location and you steer toward it. Gradually a tiny dock comes into view, and the black entry of a path leading into the woods. The wind disappears near the shore and you pull into a small plank dock. Nobody is there. You tie your painter to a small sapling just inshore from the little dock. Sitting, you carefully shift your gear onto the dock. Straightening knees stiff from kneeling on a lifejacket, you climb out and remember when this was easier.

The map shows the portage to be five hundred metres. Not having a proper yoke, you tie the paddles with the handles on the gunnels and the blades meeting near the thwart. There is now just enough space between the blades for your head. You put the lifejacket on to cushion your shoulders and hoist the canoe up, half turn, and lower it onto your back. Pushing upward on the paddles you find your balance point and shift things around, tilting the canoe up slightly at the front, and begin your portage, leaving your duffel bag and food pack by the dock. Years ago you gave up any worry about people taking your things. If people touch your gear it is only to move it off the path or keep it from sliding down a bank.

The canoe gains weight and your breath begins to come faster. Your steps are heavier.

Look out! You almost trip on a root. There are rocks and stumps underfoot. The carry is uphill, but you have gone farther and up steeper hills in the past. Birds cry unseen somewhere above you and the sun's light filters through a million holes in the emerald ceiling. Your breath gets shorter yet and muscles begin to let you know where they are and how long it has been without a rest. The ground levels and then begins a descent. Through the forest ahead your eyes finally see the sparkle of sunshine on water. Downhill and around a bend the next lake is revealed. It is small and not often used. Two planks create another tiny dock at the end of the pathway. With sudden energy you lift your canoe and hold it balanced above your head for an instant before you lower your right arm and do a half turn to gently lower it to the water. You feel almost weightless and work the stiffness out of your arms and legs. A few turns of the painter and the canoe is secured again and you walk back, seeing now the trees above you and the woodpecker flying between them. A slight breeze keeps the mosquitoes away and cools the sweat that dampens your back and armpits.

A chipmunk darts away from your worn duffel bag and food pack. Everything is lying, as always, exactly where you left it. Another chipmunk chatters at you from high in a tree. A granola wrapper lies in the path. It is the only garbage you have seen all morning and automatically you put it in your pocket.

Trudging along the trail you reunite your gear with your canoe. Time for a swim! Though you are completely alone you still look around before stripping naked in the shadows. You lay your clothes out in the sun to dry the dampness and sweat. The soft brown muck blurs when you step through it, your foot descending deeply, touching beaver sticks as you carefully wade into the deeper water. You duck below chest height and the fresh coldness steals your breath. Smooth strokes carry you away from shore. Looking underwater you dimly see old logs and stumps far below and small silver-sided fish that dart into their own weedy forest. You float languidly for a while before swimming back to shore to negotiate the rough bottom underfoot. Standing naked in the sunlight, drying yourself off, you can already see the next portage at the far end of the lake. You change into cut-offs and a T-shirt. Load the canoe again and paddle to the end of the lake.

And so continues the day. Two more small lakes and a large one. Occasionally you pass other canoeists with a friendly wave in the distance or a shouted comment about the good weather—but mostly you are alone here, alone with your thoughts, with the quietness of the woods and lakes. Late in the afternoon you scan the shorelines for the best campsite and eventually spot a tiny beach with a small, open, flat area behind. There is a smooth stony arm reaching westward into the lake. A place to sit and watch the sunset.

Your canoe gently runs up onto the sand beach and you step ashore. You explore the campsite fully. No bear scat, or litter, or poison ivy. Firewood and kindling has been left beside a small pile of rocks for a grill—simple Canadian courtesy from last week's or last month's camper. They left no other trace of their stay, and you won't either. All you smell is the lavender clean of cedar trees. Here and there are dead branches not yet claimed for firewood by earlier visitors. You gather them as you go.

Your cook fire is small and made of sweet-smelling coniferous branches. The bottom of your fry pan is black from the smoke, and the smell will be conjured back for months in the city when you reheat the old pan. But today you eat from its wholesome inside, wipe grease from it with a piece of bread, and relax on the beach with a coffee boiled from lake water.

The sun lowers. You tie a rope around a rock and spot a sturdy branch to haul the food up high and away. You miss. You try again and again and finally your weighted rope sails over the large horizontal limb while the other end plays out in your hand. You haul your food bag high and secure the other end around a tree.

Now you need another swim. Discarding your clothes again you find the sandy beach is clean and smooth for a long way out. You enter the cool clear water as the sun begins to lower toward the lake surface.

This is heaven. And this is Canada.

Driving the Highway by Susan Statham

Alan Bland

THE GREAT CANADIAN ROAD TRIP

On May 5, 2017, I had a flashback, and it wasn't due to all the fibre my doctor had recommended. I woke up to the fact that on May 5, 1993, twenty-four years before, Hunter and I had set off on a grand adventure—The Great Canadian Road Trip. Hunter being my old pal, Barry Hunter, and like me a "motor-head." When I first broached the subject of "the grand adventure," he was less than enthusiastic; in fact he was downright rude. Then I said the magic words: "In a Rolls-Royce." And Hunter was hooked. So from whence appeared the Roller? Back in the days when, as a not-so-young lad, I did some insurance brokering I got to know a shifty character in the insurance industry named Dean, who had the common sense to exit the business and set up what became a company called Canadian Movie Cars. Dean knew who owned all those old classic automobiles and would broker them out to movie, advertising and television shoots and sometimes to weddings

You see, I was about to get wed and needed something special to impress the bride and upstage her father, who was only a Cadillac guy. So I went to Dean and said, "Whatcha got?" He had old Buicks and Packards and many other brands of Detroit's many misdemeanours. And then he said the magic words, "How about a 1927 Rolls-Royce?"

Dean played chauffeur to the bride and father, got lost, and they nearly missed the ceremony, but that's another story…and my life would have been forever changed.

The F-in-law had had an interesting career as a sergeant in the Scots Guards, as a Glasgow "bobby," as a stockbroker in Toronto, and then as an impresario. And the one thing missing to complete the picture was, yep: a Rolls-Royce. By then he had moved to Vancouver but was currently visiting and depleting my supply of single malt when he said that he still wanted that Roller.

Fate played its hand. I knew that Dean was moving to Florida, something about better weather and lower taxes, and was selling his house and his own personal Rolls-Royce. And it was a beauty, a Silver Shadow with sage green lower panels and pewter upper body. Fool that I am, I asked the F-in-law if he would like to see it, and as Dean lived a stone's throw away, off we went. Well he saw it, drove it and bought the darned thing on the spot. Then took off for Vancouver while the money changed hands and the paperwork was done.

That's when the "adventure" really started. He didn't trust the car transporter companies to ship his car without dinging it. Late one evening I took a call asking me if I would drive the darned thing out to Vancouver for him. And the next day I phoned Hunter and, after being rudely abused, I had my co-pilot!

May 5, 1993, wasn't much different than May 5, 2017, cool and wet when we set off at 5:30 in the morning. We had decided to get a lot of miles done before calling it a night; we aimed for the north country and hoped to make Thunder Bay. The car was purring along and, ensconced in soft Cordovan leather seats, we were as happy as clams. With a ten-day temporary permit stuck in the window until the car could be registered in BC, we motored along just above the limit. Due to the temporary permit we decided to take the Canadian route and not cross into the States to avoid having to explain the whole story. The American route could have saved a few hundred miles, but cost how much time convincing the US customs guys that we were only in transit?

The tank was topped up before we left Port Credit with 68.9 litres at .499 cents a litre for a total of $34.38. We had a full tank and were on our way!

Finally dawn appeared, a grey and uninviting dawn, but it began to get lighter and we settled in to what could become a long and boring journey. The cachet of driving the Roller would soon wear off and we needed to keep ourselves amused. There was still lake-effect snow around and the big car was running on all-season tires, so we decided to take the northern route on Trans-Canada Highway 11 through North Bay and stay away from the southern, snowier route, Trans-Canada Highway 17.

In Latchford, north of North Bay, we pumped some more gas in the beast—91.68 litres, but now the price was .589 cents per litre for a total of $54.00, and we wondered why those Northerners drove gas-guzzling pickup trucks.

I had never understood how lonely you could feel while cruising a long stretch of highway where no other vehicles came past for an hour or so, when you were driving an eighteen-year-old car for which you couldn't find a spare part within five hundred miles. And that's when we saw the bear. A big old black bear, loping along the side of the highway. I could only imagine being broken down at the side of the highway in a rag-top, not another vehicle in sight and the bear circling the car....

But the bear wasn't interested in us and we sailed past, the Roller's near-seven-litre V8 purring along nicely; now I understood why the Battle of Britain pilots loved those old Rolls-Royce Merlins in their Spitfires and Hurricanes. I remembered how R.R. had always maintained that their cars were so quiet you could hear the clock ticking. Well, it was true; but then again maybe they put in noisy clocks.

In Hearst we put in another 82 litres for $52.00 and in Nipigon added another 76 litres for $45.57. That car just loved gas!

Finally, we rolled into Thunder Bay, a town I had visited many times, always courtesy of Air Canada, and we drove to my favourite hotel, the Valhalla, only to be turned away as they had no vacancies. Tried a couple more and had the same experience. After driving fourteen hours we were somewhat zoned out but finally asked the clerk at the Ramada, "What gives?"

To which he responded, "Stomping Tom is in town!"

"Stomping Tom?" I replied.

"Yes sir," he said, "There's not a hotel room to be had in town tonight."

Now I don't mind Stomping Tom, or "Bud the Spud," but when two guys in a Roller can't find room at the inn then something's amiss. The clerk at the Ramada was kind enough to phone around and found us a room in Kakabeka Falls, so after a gourmet dinner in Pizza Hut, we drove another hour to the Kakabeka Falls Motel.

It wasn't what I'd expected. After manoeuvering the Roller through the big rigs, pickups and Harleys, we entered through the pool hall to reach reception. The black leather, tattoos, chains and boots were interesting, and that was just on the ladies. But we were allowed to pass and reach reception where we checked in for a double. They probably thought we were undercover cops, doing a sting.

I noted the caveat on the check-in receipt: "The person registering is responsible for all damages caused to room, furnishings and fixtures." And all for $40.32 double, tax included. I was used to Hyatts and Hiltons saying you were responsible for phone and room service charges, but trashing rooms?

Having parked the Roller up to the window, we retired to our room with a bottle of Scotch. As Hunter snored the whole night away, I spent most of the time looking out at the Roller, making sure no one ripped off the Silver Lady on the hood. My fears went unfounded, probably because the locals couldn't make sense of why two townies were dangling a classic car in front of them. Either that or they were just nice folks—and I think that's just what they were, tattoos, chains and all. You live in a big city and expect the rest of the country to act by the same standards.

I thought it best to check in with SWMBO (She Who Must Be Obeyed) and asked her to let her father know that we were averaging fifteen miles per gallon, not bad considering the size of engine and that the Roller weighed close to two tons. And so to breakfast where the sign said, "Breakfast—Worms—Gas"; well, that about summed it up, and after partaking of breakfast and gas and foregoing the worms we headed west.

My Petro-Canada receipt says that we pumped in 83.7 litres at .609 cents for a total of $51.00! Do you see a trend developing here?

West from Thunder Bay to the Manitoba border has some of the most spectacular scenery in the world. But then again so does most every other part of Canada. Here again we had a choice: go the southerly route on Highway 11 through Fort Frances and then north on Highway 71 to Kenora, or take Highway 17 to Dryden, which looked shorter but less scenic. Highway 17 through Dryden won and I still wonder what we missed by not taking the longer route. The weather held sunny and mild and the sunlight sparkled off the countless lakes we passed. If only it wasn't for those winters….

A strange thing happened after we passed the Manitoba border. The scenery changed and the highway seemed to stretch out ahead of us with little to relieve the monotony. It's an odd phenomenon but flatlanders seem to like this. I remember a conversation with a lady from Saskatchewan whose family had bought a cabin in the Rockies, and after two years sold it because they felt hemmed in and missed the wide-open prairies.

So, like in the song, we motored west and finally realized the magnitude of the task we'd undertaken as mile after mile of arrow-straight highway and prairie rolled past. The monotony finally broke when the police cruiser coming toward us on the other side of the divided highway pulled a U-turn over the median, lit up his rack and we politely pulled over. Probably not having seen a Rolls-Royce before and noting the absence of a front plate, and looking for an interesting story for roll-call, he decided we were it. After reading us the riot act because our temporary permit had slipped down in the window, he let us get on our way. The most excitement he'd had since the cows busted out of old Hector's barn.

We kissed the south end of Winnipeg and gassed up the beast again; 64.39 litres and the card was hit for another $34.06.

As the old saying went, "Go west young man." But I don't think we were feeling so young anymore. So onwards to Saskatchewan. By now things were starting to get blurry, but we seemed to have gassed up in Grenfell, Saskatchewan, with 90 litres and another $51.00. I know, who cares?

Regina hove up on the horizon and it looked so close, those high-rise buildings sticking up from the billiard-table-flat prairies. An hour later they were no closer and I know we'd driven at least sixty miles. Hunter was ready with a devastating one liner: "You could sit on your front porch and watch your dog run away for days!" How right he was; another hour and those frickin' towers were still no closer.

Eventually we came up on Regina, and by that time were so sick of looking at it we blew past and headed for the next great metropolis on the prairies, Moose Jaw. Those prairie folk do have a certain gift for naming their towns, don't they?

So here we were, after two days of straight driving, in Moose Jaw, Saskatchewan, well over 1,300 miles from Toronto, and another bottle of Scotch to liberate after pumping another 89.9 litres and hitting Mr. VISA for over $50.00. We stayed at the Best Western Heritage Inn, and I knew that the trip was becoming a little too much like a *Twilight Zone* episode when Hunter got all excited because he could get Red River cereal for breakfast. It was time to move on.

I know we gassed up in Piapot (how could anyone forget that name, although it was an Anglicized version of the original, Nehiyawapot), in the middle of a vast plain that went on forever, and then some. Piapot was a famous chief of the local southern Cree tribes, but we didn't stop long enough to get the history. Since then I have checked into his past, and he was an exceptional man who led his southern Cree tribe through the horrendous period when they were forced into submission. He finally died in 1908 aged ninety-two.

But I remember the gas guy pumping into the Roller and he kept looking underneath to see if we had a leak! He said that he'd never seen a Rolls-Royce before and had never pumped that much gas into a car before either. When I told him we still had about a third of a tank when we pulled in he walked away shaking his head. That bill seems to have lost itself, but I know it was a big one at about 90 litres in an independent gas bar, so maybe that one was for cash.

And so on to Calgary. As the land began to lift, we could see the end of the flatlands. I was grateful that I could bypass Medicine Hat without stopping, having endured a winter's weekend in Medicine Hat some years previously and my car refused to start even though it had been plugged in all night. I know there are colder places on earth but I don't want to ever go there; once in Medicine Hat was enough. Calgary gas prices were a pleasant surprise as we pumped 90.2 litres at .479 cents for only $43.20!

By now we were anxious to get the job done and the car delivered, and we hadn't had a single mechanical problem to deal with. Maybe that's because Hunter had his great big red tool box in the trunk. Prepared for anything! So we blew past Dead Man's Flats, Banff, and Yoho and Glacier National Parks without a single photo shoot. Then we tackled Rogers Pass and watched the gas gauge spinning down as the two-tonne Roller wheezed up the gradient and Japanese econo-boxes buzzed past us. After that humiliation we called it a night in Revelstoke at the Sandman Inn. And it didn't take the Sandman long to get me to sleep that night, notwithstanding Hunter's stentorian snoring. In the morning I stood outside in the chilly dawn and took in the magnificent scenery and the cool clear air; it was a magic moment.

But we knew that my F-in-law was waiting anxiously to take delivery of his dream car, so on we went to Kamloops and then down the famous Coquihalla Highway to Vancouver. And it seemed that the last part of the journey we were continually stopping to gas the beast: 71.8 litres in Revelstoke and then another 47.25 litres in Langley and finally, not wishing to leave him a car running on fumes, 60 more on Granville Street in Vancouver, a few minutes from the finish line.

Hunter and I delivered the beast with not a scratch on it and I had the final words. "You know, John, when Samantha phoned you and said we were only getting fifteen miles a gallon?" He nodded sagely.

"Well, we were wrong."

John breathed a sigh of relief. "Thank God," he said.

"No, it wasn't fifteen. It was twelve!"

And then I had to explain how much the beast used getting through the Rockies. When I finally did the math we had burned about 206 gallons and driven 2,553 miles, and all in three-and-a-half days. So we actually came in at about 12.5 miles per gallon. Forget all that litres-per-100-kilometres nonsense; this was a British car, after all.

John had some good years out of that car and when I visited, it was always available to me. The last time I drove it was for a sad occasion, in the funeral procession of his wife and my mother-in-law, Helen. I had three lovely elderly ladies in the car, and I'm sure that as we drove through the streets of Vancouver, they all raised their lace-gloved hands and gave a little wave to passers-by.

Felicity Sidnell Reid

THIS LEAF

This leaf—
a green parakeet
perched on corpses
leached grey-blue
in November's rain
ghosts of summer
and drifting days
of scarlet and gold.
But shriek
all you like—
I'm green, I'm green!
You'll come to this,
unhappy leaf,
a grey skeleton
in winter's grip
stamped into soil.
Yet under the snow,
winter wheat grows
luminous green.
A living tide
flowing between
winter and spring.

Hanging On by Alan Langford

Kim Grove

A LETTER FROM ON BOARD THE SHIP *SPEEDY*

This is a fictional piece that imagines what John Fisk might have been thinking, the day before the Speedy *capsized off the coast of Brighton, Ontario, while sailing from York to Newcastle, now Toronto to Presqu'ile Point.*

John Fisk was High Constable of York, the first Canadian police officer killed in the line of duty in Ontario. The ship was carrying both a prisoner and those who would try the case of a trapper who had been killed. The first trial in the area was intended to establish the importance of the Newcastle settlement. However, after the ship sank with all hands, plans to make Newcastle the capital of Upper Canada were discarded.

October 7, 1804

My Darling,

I hope you know that I love you. We get betoiled by the cares of the farm some days that I forget to tell you how I feel.

This voyage on the *Speedy* has made me uneasy. Perhaps it is the constant chatter of the boys on the crew who talk of its lack of seaworthiness. At times I see water lunge over the sides. The breakers lift the ship up so high. I've heard Captain Paxton curse with fear more than once under his breath as the boat heaves and then lets out a creaking sound, instead of a sigh, as it tries to steady itself atop of the waves.

For whatever reason this short time away has brought back memories of heading off to fight in the Revolutionary War. There was the anticipation of adventure mixed with the threat of deadly danger. Yet I was younger then. I was able to shift the apprehension to think I was indestructible. Now, the dark clouds o'er head and the rough slapping of the waves make me less courageous and more focused on home.

I know this was the worst time for me to be taking this trip, what with harvest needing tending to and all, but our boys have shown clear signs of being men now and I'm sure they will be able to manage 'til I get back. A hard day's work never hurt anyone.

My task in guarding the prisoner has been no hardship. He sits in his cell, silent, hardly eating. The interpreter on board, George Cowan, said the only thing Ogetonicut has said is that upon his death he wants the necklace around his neck to be given to his son. Either he admits his guilt with this request or as a Native he has no trust in our justice system and knows Justice Thomas Cochran will pronounce him guilty. Whichever, I find it an unusual situation. There is nothing about this man that is similar to other criminals that have been under my charge. There is no yelling or moving in the cell like an angry bull. Instead he lies on his bed staring at the wall. He is calm, almost too calm. There are rumours among the crew that Ogetonicut did not murder the trapper. They say it was another trapper who killed John Sharpe for his pelts and made it look like the work of a member of the Ojibway tribe.

It will be a good test of this new district of Newcastle to have such a trial there. I don't have much to do with the others on the *Speedy* as I can't leave the prisoner, except when I'm relieved to sleep. But it's hard to sleep when the boat does constantly rise as though heading for Heaven and then plunges as though pulled back toward Hell.

There is too much uncertainty on this voyage—uncertainty of the trial, of the weather, of this boat, and those upon it. So much uncertainty has made it more important to write you now, putting this letter in a bottle, in case I never make it to shore to put it in the post. There is one thing I am certain of; I love you, truly.

Your loving husband,

John Fisk

Peggy Dymond Leavey

THE LOST KENTÉ MISSION

In 1668 the Quebec-based Order of St. Sulpice sent three young priests to establish a Christian mission to the Cayuga (Iroquois) people living in the area known as Kenté. The Bay of Quinte region of eastern Ontario is today generally referred to as Quinte. But in earlier times it was called Kenté or Canta, from a native word meaning "a stopping place," or "a place to go forward." Kenté comprised a vast region that would stretch today from east of Deseronto to west of Cobourg, to north of Belleville and south into Prince Edward County.

Travelling by canoe from Lachine against the current of the St. Lawrence, it took Fathers Trouvé, Fenélon and D'Urfé twenty-six days to reach their final destination. The mission would most probably have been headquartered in one of the larger villages in Kenté, where too the leading men or chiefs would have lived.

Once settled, the priests began their work, setting forth on a wilderness circuit, ministering to the natives in villages all along the north shore of Lake Ontario. Early records show that Father D'Urfé spent a winter hunting and fishing at Ganaraska (near present-day Port Hope). He left the Kenté Mission in 1674.

Father Fenélon appears to have travelled farther afield; Fenelon Falls is named in his honour. Apparently, Fenélon had a dispute with the Comte de Frontenac, the governor of French Canada, and was ordered back to France. Other Sulpicians may have subsequently joined Father Trouvé, who remained at the mission until 1680 when it closed.

Financial support for the Kenté Mission dwindled after Frontenac chose Cataraqui (Kingston) as the site for his fort on Lake Ontario. Religious conversion of the First Nations people had not been a great success, and the Cayugas began searching for new hunting grounds anyway, eventually returning to their ancient homeland in the Finger Lakes district of New York State.

In 1687 those natives who had stayed behind at Kenté were attacked by French soldiers under orders from the governor, the Marquis de Denonville, and his native allies, who were hostile to the Iroquois. While the inhabitants of the village were sleeping, the enemy swept in and captured the chiefs, taking them back to Fort Frontenac, where some were tortured before being sent to France to serve as galley slaves.

When Frontenac resumed the governorship of French Canada, after de Denonville was recalled to France, he returned to this country in 1689 and was said to have brought with him one of the captured chiefs, who then made his way back to the scene of the treachery. The man found the village of Kenté empty, the mission abandoned. The inhabitants had vanished, and over the ensuing years the whereabouts of the mission became shrouded in mystery.

***

In the little village of Consecon there is today a historical marker that tells the story of "The Lost Mission to the Cayuga people … generally thought to have been located in the Consecon area." Some historians were of the opinion that Kenté may have been a movable town, following the First Nations' custom of resettling in a different but nearby location every ten to fifteen years, thus making it impossible to pinpoint. But there was one man who, 270 years later, set out to find its exact location and to prove its existence, once and for all.

Bowen P. Squire was born in Hendon, England, in 1901. Both his parents were American citizens, although his father, a Baptist preacher, had been posted to England, and it was there that Bowen was born and where he received his early education.

When Bowen was fourteen the family came to live in Ontario, Canada, near Carrying Place, the ancient portage road between Wellers Bay, which is an arm of eastern Lake Ontario, and the Bay of Quinte.

Bowen was interested in history, even then. He listened to the stories of the old people, descendants of the first Loyalist settlers to the area. They told of sites where native artifacts had been found, evidence of people who lived in or passed through the region, long before the arrival of the Europeans.

The youth also got to know George Chadd, an employee of the Central Ontario Railroad who worked at the Carrying Place station. Chadd was an ardent collector of artifacts, displaying a variety of pottery sherds, arrowheads, and stone tools in his home museum. Every day after his regular work the man would go looking for more of these treasures.

Young Bowen Squire was intrigued by Chadd's avocation and began to do some digging of his own, discovering that some finds were buried deep beneath the soil, while others lay very near the surface, already disturbed by the farmer's plough.

Although keenly interested in archaeology, Bowen Squire never formally studied it, choosing instead to study art. (Today, his historical paintings of daily life among the United Empire Loyalists and scenes of First Nations people hang in private collections and museums in Canada and the US.) He taught Biblical history in college and, after doing some preaching in Bronte, Ontario, and Toronto, he was posted to the US where he took up the ministry in 1927.

Married in 1930, Bowen Squire worked for the US government during WWII. After the war, while he and his wife and young son were living in Rhode Island, he wrote to a real estate agent back in Carrying Place. He was looking for a one-hundred-acre farm on a lake, preferably with a mature maple tree out front. The real estate agent found the perfect place, and Squire bought it, sight unseen. In 1946, he arrived back in the Quinte area, now with a wife and son.

Reverend Squire became the minister of the Baptist Church in Crofton, near Mountain View, in Prince Edward County. For fourteen years he also gave art lessons in Trenton and at his home. He continued to pursue his interest in archaeology, writing papers for universities and societies and giving lectures on his favourite topic three or four times a week.

An authority on First Nations remains, he would sometimes be asked by the Ontario Provincial Police to determine the age and origin of skeletons they'd found. It was nothing for him to have a pile of bones to sort through on the kitchen table.

While studying local history to help with his paintings and illustrations, he formed a theory about Allisonville, or Pearsall, Creek that cuts across Prince Edward County, connecting the waters of Long Reach (west of the entrance to Hay Bay) in the east, through Consecon Lake, to Lake Ontario via Wellers Bay in the west.

Today, Consecon Lake is about six miles long and one mile wide, twice the size it was before 1806 when a dam was built to hold back the water. Prior to that, it was not much more than a wider, deeper section of the creek.

In Squire's opinion, that creek would have provided the early Iroquois, fleeing the Hurons and the French, a secure route of travel, much safer than trying to navigate around the rugged shoreline of Prince Edward County, battling the waves of Lake Ontario.

The Archaeological and Historic Sites Board of Ontario, aware of Bowen Squire's interest and expertise, asked him to aid in the quest for the lost Kenté Mission. They also helped get him a small grant toward his expenses.

Using copies of original Jesuit recollects and old records from British museums he began his search. Records told of the Kenté Mission being so many days west of Fort Frontenac. If Squire's theory of the interior route was correct, there should be evidence of village sites along the creek.

In time, Squire found the pattern of closely allied villages he was looking for, each site three or four hours travel time from the next—regular "stopping places." Within a ten-mile radius of Consecon Lake itself he found evidence of six large villages, four smaller ones, and a number of burial sites.

Squire was always quick to admit that he was not the "discoverer" of all the sites; the location of some had been known for generations, and many had been well picked over in the past. He only tried to uncover them again and fit them into his scheme.

The largest site in the group and the most central was on the north side of Consecon Lake, on the property that had been owned by the Squires for the past five years. It was the only village in the group that had not been discovered by early collectors. Perhaps on a hunch, this is where he began.

After some searching of the surface, excavations began on this site in 1951, and a year later the first evidence was found, in a midden, or rubbish heap. While he worked, Squire carefully charted and recorded all his finds—stone pipes, slate beads, fragments of fire stones, stone medicine bowls, and stone and flint scrapers, to mention only a few.

In 1953 he reported the Squire site to the curator of the National Museum in Ottawa, and Thomas Lee, the museum's field representative, came to help identify many of the artifacts.

Lee considered the site—half a mile long, three-quarters of a mile wide—to have had at its centre a pallisaded town at one time. With the lake in front and quick sand swamps on three sides, its defence would not have been a problem. Its position on a promontory affording a clear view of Wellers Bay, the Carrying Place portage, and the entrance to the Trent Valley would have made it the ideal observation post for a First Nations chief.

If the Cayugas had settled in each village in the grouping for the customary period of time, each location taking them closer to Lake Ontario and their home in New York State, the order of migration would have placed them at the Squire site during the period that the Kenté Mission was active.

University of Toronto professor T.F. McIlwraith, president of the Archaeological and Historic Sites Board of Ontario, spent some time at the Squire site, later writing that he was "convinced" that here was the site of the lost mission, the largest part of which was now buried under the water of Consecon Lake.

On June 21, 1956, the *Globe and Mail* described Squire's find as "one of the most exciting collections of these ancient relics in Ontario and possibly in Canada."

Dr. Law of Queen's University toured the site, and archaeology students and summer tourists alike were attracted to what was the largest find to date in eastern Canada. Bowen Squire had hoped his site could be developed in the same way as Sainte-Marie among the Hurons at Midland. Professor Wilfred Jury, working at Huronia with a government grant, shared Squire's dream of the day when there would be a historic site at both ends of the Trent-Severn system, showing the movement of the First Nations people.

But that was not to be. In spite of interest by many professors and experts from Ottawa's Museum of Man, Squire was unable to get support from any level of government. He offered to give the site to the government, free of charge, if they would agree to open his log house as a museum. Still, no interest.

After living on the site for twenty years, Rev. Bowen P. Squire, totally disheartened, sold the one-hundred-acre farm. Within hours of the sale being finalized, representatives from both federal and provincial governments drove up the lane toward his house. They wanted the property. But they were too late.

The new owner was not interested in the site's historic significance, and the farmer's first order of business was to plough the fertile soil and get his crop into the ground. Time and tide wait for no man.

Maureen Mullally

RAIN

My husband, two little ones and I had been reunited for almost a month in our new country after being separated by the Atlantic Ocean for three. Now the days were passing so quickly; so much was happening, so much had happened already. Here I was with a new job, child care arranged, my husband's work hours and mine staggered to fit into a schedule for all of us.

My last customer was under the dryer. She would be combed out and ready to go by nine, our closing time today. I hoped she had brought her rain hat, and umbrella. This rain didn't look as though it would stop any time soon.

The Beginning - 1954

Rose, my boss, invited me to have a coffee with her before we cleaned up. I was getting used to her continual coffee drinking. We relaxed for a few minutes and discussed the events of the day.

"Mrs. Miller said she knew I was Irish before I had even given her my name," I told Rose.

"Well I hope you didn't tell her any different, she never likes to be wrong," she replied.

"Oh no, the customer is always right," I said. "That's one of the first things I learned when I was doing my apprenticeship at Selfridges in London."

We were all tidied up and finished for the day shortly after nine. Rose locked up and we went on our opposite ways home.

What a rain storm! Within seconds my umbrella had blown inside out. I tied my rain hat on tighter and wished I had worn my flat-heeled shoes, not my special red three-inch heels. They would be ruined in all this rain. The street was like a small river. The only thing I could do was to take them off. So that's what I did. I paddled through the rushing rain water the rest of the way home in my nylon stockings.

"Wow, it really, really rains in Canada," I thought. Fortunately, I was home in thirty minutes.

My husband had fed and bathed our two little ones. He was glad to see me. What a fright I must have looked, wet-through and bedraggled. But my red shoes were dry and saved. Granny had bought them for me, my chosen parting gift before we left England. Red leather "sling back, peep toe, high heels." I just loved them.

The next day we received anxious telegrams from family in England. Were we safe? Were we affected?

They had heard of the devastation Hurricane Hazel had caused. People and buildings swept away, hundreds drowned, and so on. Since we had no radio or television, we were totally unaware of the situation: what had occurred—and what we had lived through. How fortunate we were. We were so close to the disaster zones—four hundred people were evacuated from the nearby trailer park, which had been totally destroyed.

It was estimated damages were in the 100-million-dollar range (in the billions today).

Four thousand families were left homeless.

Thirty-two homes were washed away in one street alone.

Homes were ripped from their foundations and swept into the lake.

There were many other disasters and many heroes as well.

Yes it did "really, really" rain in Canada on October 15, 1954.

And what happened to the red shoes?

Well, I still have them. I can no longer wear them of course; three-inch heels at my age would be a bit too much! But like Dorothy's red shoes in the *Wizard of Oz*, they brought me home—to Canada.

James Ronson

FLOOD

Jenny knew the family never talked about the flood. It had something to do with the man her Gran was living with at the time. The man who would have been her grandfather.

But when the teacher said they had to do some research on a local history project, Jenny couldn't resist. It was like one of those science projects where the iron filings form a pattern round the poles. The flood was like a magnetic pole to her. It dragged her in.

Plus she had questions. She always had questions. Most of them never answered. Like the time back in Grade 5 two years ago when she overheard her mom talking to one of her girlfriends and her mom had called her birth father a sperm donor. Afterwards she had asked her mom, "What's a sperm donor?" and her mom had given her a look that could freeze lakes and told her that she wasn't supposed to hear that. She knew what it was now, of course, but Mom still wouldn't talk about it.

Her mom wasn't due home for another half hour from her job delivering the mail in town. And even if Jenny did beat her home, her mom would know she was probably at the library. Jenny loved the library. The library was the place where you could get questions answered. Once she had asked Lisa, the children's librarian, about why the Port Hope library was called a Carnegie library. Lisa just smiled and told her to look up Andrew Carnegie on the computers upstairs. So she made the trek up the stairs and logged in and checked it out on the Internet. Turned out this Carnegie was like this huge zillionaire from the States who made all this money way back in the nineteenth century, and then felt guilty about it and gave it all away to build things like this very building she was in now.

Not everyone in the library was welcoming though. In fact, Apollonia in Reference was a little scary. She was a big woman with a daffodil-bulb nose and dark black glasses. She always wore these enormous wrap-around scarfs about her neck and she didn't seem to like kids much. Jenny swallowed hard and stepped up to the desk. "Hi. I have this local history project to do at school and I was hoping you could help me."

No smile like Lisa. "What subject?"

"It's on the flood."

"Which flood? The most recent one here in Port Hope? In 1980?"

"Yeah, I guess." Jenny was trying to do the math in her head but it was too hard.

"How old are you?"

What did that have to do with the flood? she wondered, but didn't ask. "I'm twelve," she replied.

"You're small for your age."

"So I've been told." She was not trying to be impertinent. Gran's word. But she got a frown from Apollonia anyway. This wasn't going too good, she thought.

"Have you ever used the Reference Room before?"

"Uh, no. But I'm a fast learner." She remembered to smile when she said that.

"Well, okay. Please follow me and I will show you what we have." Apollonia reached into the cabinet and pulled out a file marked "Flood." "Now we have a lot of precious books in here. Please confine your research to this one file and don't touch anything else. Can you do that?" The woman narrowed her eyes and loomed over Jenny.

"Yes ma'am." That seemed to satisfy her.

"Very well. I will leave you to it. You can put the file on my desk when you are done."

"I can write stuff down in my notebook. Right?"

"Yes, you may do that," said Apollonia, tossing the words over her shoulder on the way out.

Jenny opened the file and read. The most recent flood happened on March 21, 1980. So that was what? Twenty-five years ago? But the 1980 deluge was just one in a long history of floods. In fact, in one flood back in 1890 a child even lost its life. She also learned that the floods were "partially caused by the deforestation along the banks of the Ganaraska River." So global warming may not have been as big a factor as it was in this century, but deforestation certainly was.

Ms. Chang, her teacher, would like that fact. She was all about this climate change stuff. Jenny added that thought to her notes too.

When Jenny finished reading the two newspaper articles, she switched to looking at the pictures. Wow. There were buildings damaged and water everywhere. All the way down Queen Street past the library and into the park the water coursed. Then across the street and right out into the lake. The next few pictures she looked at showed the worst damage was on Walton, the main street in town. Water everywhere. Destroyed buildings, crumbling sidewalks. What a mess.

She focused more intently on one of the pictures and that was then she saw it. The sign for Atwater Antiques. The front window shattered. Water everywhere outside and in.

She had always thought it a funny name. Atwater. Though she never dared to laugh about it. That was *his* name, Gran told her. Her mom's father. The guy who would have been her grandfather. First name Richard but otherwise known as Dick. Dick disappeared in the middle of the night and was never seen by the family again.

It was a small part of the untold story that Gran had revealed one day a year or so back. Gran explained that she took pictures of the damage the next day after the flood. That was for the insurance rider they were supposed to have, but didn't. What little money they had went out in the ATM that night courtesy of Dick. The bank wasn't in the flood plain, added Gran. "Took the goddamn truck too and left me with nothing. Nothing but your mother. She was about the same age as you are now. Then he left me alone to raise your mom in that cramped little apartment above the store. Had to sell what was left at discount prices just to try and pay the rent. Wasn't much call for antiques back then, so I had to sell everything including the store." Then her mom came home and Gran never talked about it again.

Jenny shuffled through the rest of the photos. None triggered the memories like Atwater did, though she did find three she decided to photocopy for her report. Of course, she left the library with more unanswered questions.

As Jenny crossed the black iron bridge she threw a glance down at the roiling river. It was hard to imagine such destruction lay in something as natural as that. But it was when she reached the other side she saw the sign. Always read the signs, her mom said. In Jenny's experience, most people simply ignored them. Yet there it was. After the great flood a re-channelling and a deepening of the river had taken place to avoid future disasters. She needed to know when that had happened for her report. And now she did know. The year was 1985.

Jenny crossed Mill Street and climbed the concrete steps up the steep hill to King Street. King Street was known for being the street where the famous author Farley Mowat lived. They had read his book *Owls in the Family* back in Grade 5.

At the big historical blue house she turned left onto her street, Dorset Street East. When she was talking to people around town, her mom often left the East part out just to get a rise out of people. This was because the other street in town where the rich people lived was Dorset Street West. And the fact was there was no connection between the two, none whatsoever. Her mom was fully aware of that, of course, being a postie and all. She knew every street in town.

There were two massive mansions spilling out onto Dorset East that looked like they belonged on King Street. They stuck out like a pair of dress shoes on a guy wearing shorts. The rest of the houses on the south side of Dorset East were as small and ordinary as they come, and none more so than hers. Her house was farther down near Princess. Now that was something she knew she would never be called! As in, a princess. Usually such words came from older guys and Jenny had always lived in a house surrounded by women. Her mom Kate. Her Gran Louise. And Jenny. Always just the three.

There was a retirement home on the street as well. Gran liked to joke that it would be a really short move when she was ready. Just a short shuffle across the street with her suitcase and her walker.

The arrival of men through the revolving front door for one-night stands or boyfriends of the month appeared to have fallen off of late. Her mom had given up smoking two years ago and she seemed to have done the same with men. Jenny had trouble understanding the attraction of either. These days Mom didn't talk too much about men and didn't seem to like them much either.

And therein lay Jenny's problem. The subject of men. Past men. Biologically speaking, they were half the reason why Jenny was even here. The half that was never talked about.

Her teacher had said that the class couldn't just Google the answers to their questions about their project. Secondary sources were a must. Hence her visit to the library. Well, that part was the easy one. Now came the hard part. The class also needed to talk directly to at least two people in town about what they remembered. And for Jenny those two people were Gran and Mom.

As she picked her way along the street she wondered when and how to broach the subject of the flood. Right away? Or after supper? Singly or together?

She finally decided both together over dessert and coffee. Jenny had only joined the coffee club since turning twelve. This despite being told by Gran who had been told by her mother that it would stunt her growth. "Why do you think we are all so small? It's this stuff," she said, and poured herself another cup.

Supper tonight was roast chicken. Always good. Jenny could feel the coil of the notebook she'd shoved under her bum all through dinner. Gran talked about her day at the bakery downtown. She nearly always had a story or two to tell. The great thing about the bakery was it closed after four, so all three of them were always home for dinner and it gave Gran lots of time to cook. When dinner was done Jenny got up to clear the plates and left her notebook lying on the chair.

Well, of course her mom noticed it right away. "What are you doing, silly, sitting there on your notebook?" And as Mom reached for the notebook, the three photocopies fluttered to the floor. Mom stooped to pick them up before Jenny could get back to the table. Thumbing through the pictures, she glanced at Jenny. "What are these all about?"

Whoops. Now Jenny had no choice but to jump in head first. "They're for my project. It's on the Port Hope flood of 1980. I was just at the library and I found that one of Walton Street during the flood and what do you know, there was a picture of Atwater Antiques."

Silence.

"And um. I know I'm not…I mean I know that you, you and Gran don't want to talk about it and all that, but the teacher said I needed to talk about my subject to at least two people in town and who else can I ask except you and Gran?" There, she had said it. All at once a river of tears clouded her eyes she looked over at her mom and noticed her mom's eyes were starting to glisten too. Seconds later there were rivulets running down her mother's cheeks.

Her mom wiped her eyes with the back of her hand. "Okay, Jenny. I guess it's time. And don't get me wrong, it's not you, it's me. Please, sit down."

Jenny slouched down in the chair and looked at her mother.

"First of all, I know I should have talked about your father a long time ago." Her mom hesitated and looked away.

"You mean the one you called my sperm donor?"

"Yes, that one." Her mom's lips were trembling. She reached out her arms. Ever so slowly Jenny rose from her chair, stepped toward her and knelt in front of her. "I'm really, really sorry about that," her mom said.

"I know."

Several moments of silence. "Mom? Can I ask you something now?"

"Yes, Jenny."

"Do you, do you at least remember his name?"

Her mom sighed deeply. "His name was Mark. He worked as a tree planter up north. I met him at the hotel. It lasted, well, a few weekends. I honestly don't have any idea where he is now. He often talked about working the oil rigs out west." Mom's eyes were trickling again. "I was young, Jenny. As you know. I never had much luck with men. But I've been trying. Trying lately just to focus on you. On being a good single parent."

"I know, Mom." Jenny reached for her and pulled her close.

"It's good to hear you say that," her mom said. Deep sigh. The world stopped and Jenny could feel them both breathing as one. At long last they were interrupted by a voice.

"Here." It was Gran with a box of Kleenex.

They broke apart. Each took a tissue and dried her eyes at the same time. Jenny looked at her mom. To Jenny's surprise, she was actually smiling. "Now I don't know how much of what I just said you could use in your project, but it is something you deserved to know."

Jenny nodded. "Thanks, Mom. I know that was hard for you."

Her mom nodded, and then each of them slipped back into the two chairs at the table. Gran spoke again. "Now maybe, just maybe, I can give you something you can use in that report of yours. I awoke alone in the middle of the night to the sound of rushing water and broken glass. Your mother was asleep in the other bedroom next door."

Jenny began to write.

Richard M. Grove

SOME SORT OF NORMAL

Mark and Frank sat at a picnic table in the back yard of Aunt Miriam's house. "We were just normal kids, weren't we?" Mark said. "Weird family, but nonetheless us kids were some sort of normal. I think we all grew up kind of normal, but who really knows what lurks below the surface? We even fought like normal kids."

Frank laughed and poked Mark in the ribs. "I know I was normal, but you I am not so sure about. I remember one time when I threw a small piece of wood at you. Who knows why? It whizzed through the air like our orange Frisbee. It was kind of like throwing a stone at a bird, but not really expecting to hit it, and you never do, but it hit you right between the eyes, and it cut open your forehead, and you bled like a stuck pig. You squealed like one too, you sissy. Mother sent Jimmy out to see what the ruckus was all about. He came running from the house thinking that I must have tried to kill you with an axe or something because there was so much crying and blood. You got blood all over your hands and all over your shirt and up the wall on the way in the house. Dripping spots led a path all the way to the bathroom. Oh man, you howled like a wounded dog. All I wished is that you would just shut up and stop your screaming. Later on, our neighbour said that she almost called for an ambulance you were screaming so loud. You wouldn't have known it was just a little scratch and didn't need stitches. Everyone was pissed off at me for days. Mother screamed at me, 'It could have been so much worse. You could have put an eye out. Don't you think before you act?' I paid for that big time.

"I think that we were pretty normal kids. We used to bike all over the place. The three of us. Jim was the youngest, so I tied a rope from my bike to his, and I towed him around wherever we went. Sometimes we would take a pack of wieners with us and make a fire down at the creek and stay all afternoon, swimming and lying in the sun.

"Do you remember the time when we biked all the way up to cousin Bobby's house, and I towed Jimmy up the hill at the water reservoir? We all bulleted down the other side like mad demons and I didn't think to disconnect Jimmy before heading down. I whipped out at the bottom and poor Jimmy came flyin' like a bat out of hell and landed right on top of me and my bike. His bike landed right on my nuts—I thought that I was goin' to die. I was so bruised and hurtin' I decided to call Dad to come and get us, but he was too drunk to drive, so we walked all the way home 'cause I hurt too much. Dad was always drunk in those days. It was just normal to see him drunk. Man was I sorry I ever pulled that stunt."

Mark slapped his hands on his legs and laughed out loud. "I always wondered why we were walkin' our bikes home. You just kept telling me to shut up and keep walkin'. By the time we got home it was dark, and we got hell from Mom, and Dad gave us a lickin' with his belt. Lucky he was so drunk that he could hardly swing his belt. We all just went to bed without any dinner."

Frank fell back into his chair. "Those were the days of innocence, man. Those were the days of blameless forgiveness. We were just normal kids doing normal shit. Now that we're adults we have so much to worry about, and how we can give our kids that same life of blameless innocence? Those were the good old days."

Eric E. Wright

THE MAN WHO FLEW UNDER LONDON BRIDGE

How did a man born to a farming family in Midland, Ontario, become known to his friends in the First World War as the daredevil who flew under London Bridge? That man, christened Alfred John Wright in 1890, was my father. I knew him as "Pop." His friends and business colleagues called him A.J. Knowing him thirty years later, you would never imagine that his placid exterior hid a restless drive and adventurous spirit.

Like most war veterans, he was notoriously tight-lipped about his exploits. As his youngest, I knew nothing about his war years. To me he exhibited British reserve in spades. What I have learned about his early years has been pieced together from photos he took, letters to my mother, research in the archives, and the recollections of my older cousins.

Sometime toward the end of the nineteenth century, his family left their farm in Midland to drive their cattle and transport their possessions to a new farm in the rich agricultural land southwest of Kitchener, Ontario. Imagine calming recalcitrant cattle, resistant pigs, and cackling chickens terrified by passing "tin lizzies" during their 140-mile odyssey along country roads and through villages.

Once settled near Washington, Ontario—a village now non-existent on modern maps—Alfred attended high school. He next enrolled in the University of Toronto, from which he graduated as an engineer.

With the German kaiser rattling his sabre in Europe, Britain appealed for volunteers from subjects all over the empire. Like many young men of his day, a sense of duty to God, king, and country led him to join the Canadian militia.

Meanwhile, up the road about three miles from the Wrights, the Andrew Hall clan worked their family farm. Among the children were three girls and three boys. But it was Agnes Hall, born in 1889, who caught his eye. A primary teacher, she taught in various schools around the area. For a couple of years she even taught grades 1 through 8 in a one-room schoolhouse in Washington, quite near the Wright farm. After school, I am told, she often hoped that her father would pick her up with his horse and bring her home. Or did she linger to meet Alfred?

It doesn't take much to imagine Alfred squiring her to one of the local shindigs, playing tennis with her on the Hall clay court, joining her at church, or perhaps escorting her home after school. If the romantic letters that flew between them over the ensuing months and years are any indication, both were smitten—deeply. As with many young couples of that era, war intervened.

On July 28, 1914, the war to end all wars was declared. The appeal for volunteers became more urgent. Already an engineer and a member of the militia, Alfred was quickly recruited to drill men being sent off to the front. Stationed in Toronto, Alfred struggled, his sense of duty vying with his love for Agnes. On October 10, 1914, they announced their engagement.

In July of 1915, unable to wait any longer for a commission in the Royal Canadian Engineers, he joined the 4th Battalion of Infantry as part of the Canadian Overseas Expeditionary Force.

By candlelight, he wrote regularly to Agnes of ordinary events, her parcels, his dreams of her, and how much he loved her. His letters were very romantic—a side of him that I had not known. Actual events often proved too horrific to describe to sweethearts back home.

Neither romance nor career would divert him from his patriotic duty. During rare visits to the Hall family farm, Alfred and Agnes talked long into the night, sharing their hopes and dreams. Agnes suggested they maintain a link by praying for each other at a certain time each day.

Impatient, late in 1915 he went to Ottawa to join the engineers. He was quickly shipped off to England for more intense training and then to the French front. Agnes was left to watch the mail, to join other women in wrapping bandages for the forces, and to run bazaars to raise money for the Red Cross.

Details of my dad's training and exploits from September 1915 through 1916 are confusing or non-existent, probably due to the blanket of secrecy thrown over the war effort. General descriptions from that period hint at the appalling suffering and terrible casualties the Allies endured.

In November of 1916 he wrote from France about leaving his dugout on the front and riding twenty-three miles with his buddy. They had to report for interviews concerning the flying corps:

We got our billets and our horses fixed up and went out to find supper. What a time we had. Finally, we found a place full of drinking and eating soldiers…we were waited on to a plate of boiled bacon, beans, cabbage and potatoes with a hunk of bread. Then to top it off we had canned cherries.

[The next morning] we went to the Royal Flying Corps Interviewing Officer. He asked all manner of questions and…I was told I had passed and as is the custom, I had to return to my unit for a couple of weeks before being called up. Then I go as observer for a month on trial. If found satisfactory, I go on for my pilot's certificate. If not I must return to my unit.

After they returned to their unit to await instructions, he added, "Then I had to walk through the mud five or six miles to my dugout."

(This was letter no. 77 written to Agnes!)

In the letters I've been able to find, he didn't spend time writing about conditions at the front except to say, "The guns pounded away." His nonchalant style glossed over most of the horrors of trench warfare. Besides, he didn't want to add to his love's anxiety. And, as an officer, he probably escaped the worst miseries of trench warfare.

His selection to become a pilot took time. Like much of army life, it was "hurry up and wait." One report from that time commented, "An almost ideal combination for an Aviator is that obtaining in a man who has had a British public education, a good all-round engineering training, and has outdoor sporting tendencies." Except for the sporting tendencies, my dad fit the bill in spades. No wonder he was selected.

Early in 1917, he was sent back to England to receive pilot training. During a holiday he describes "civvies" gathering to watch flight training:

There were large crowds watching the flying and to amuse them there was a forced landing in a field of growing grain and another into a fence. In the latter case the machine was all smashed to pieces but no one hurt much. It all reminds me of accounts of the Roman gladiator days. They [the crowd] just hope something exciting will happen.

With so many crashes, intact machines were in short supply. As a result, Alfred describes his colleagues amusing themselves with tennis between parades and machine gun practice. He calls this period "*an extravagant waste of precious time when our friends are giving their blood away in France.*"

When the First World War began, flight was in its infancy. Only eleven years had elapsed since the Wright Brothers invented the airplane and took it for its first successful flight in 1903. Most early aircraft were flimsy and frail. Equipment failures and accidents proved as deadly as enemy gunfire. In my dad's archives he has dozens of pictures of flipped and crashed machines.

Upon hopping into the cockpit, most pilots had a life expectancy of mere weeks. Nevertheless, Canada had among its ranks many of the deadliest air aces of the war. These included Billy Bishop and Raymond Collishaw. Indeed, the top four Canadian aces accounted for 230 enemy planes—a record no other four fliers among the Allies equalled.

Ultimately Alfred received his pilot's certificate as a member of the Royal Flying Corps (RFC). Canada did not have its own air force at that time, but at least a third of the members in the RFC were Canadian. Over 22,000 served with the British flying services and almost 14,000 as aircrew. There were at least 1,388 Canadian casualties, plus 1,130 who were injured.

Successful flights depended mainly on the skill and instincts of the pilots—and divine providence. While receiving training in July 1917, my dad wrote:

Dearest Agnes,

I was sent here for a three-day course in aerial fighting. No sooner had the six of us, two from each squadron, arrived than a friend of mine from Doncaster crashed his machine through the roof of a hanger. It was his second solo. He was badly cut up and burned and died a couple of hours later. I was glad I didn't see it….Last night I was sent up to stunt [fight tactics] in a machine that only had a little petrol. I did one loop and was getting ready for another when my engine stopped at 4000 feet up. I tried all the way down to get it going … and nearly crashed…I prayed to land…and a most marvelous thing happened. I made a good landing in a wheat field at the edge of the drome, went through a low hedge without turning on its nose and stopped up in the drome without breaking anything.

Then this morning I lost myself in a ground mist within a couple of miles of the drome and I prayed again to get the machine back safely. Within less than ten minutes of that, I found the drome and landed. What a Father we have looking after us, Agnes!

By August of 1917, he was sent to France where he was attached to the 25 Squadron. He writes: *I was so fortunate for this is a dandy squadron…My work will be of the very best, in the best type of machine too….I still take your picture with me and hope never to forget it…remembering how you love me.*

His machine was probably a de Havilland that he affectionately called PAN after the call letters.

In mid-August he writes of his first trip over the line to "*engage the Huns*" and of a pilot managing to land his shot-up machine on his aerodrome before he died. A week later he writes of "*bombing Hunland,*" which he describes as "*dropping pills*"—rather cavalier terms. He says, "[*A*]*s far as I know, only one Fritz came anywhere near us.*" He writes of going on patrol four miles up "*alongside of Hunland where my observer got his face frozen a little…then we found our way home and landed safely in a strong wind at dusk when you couldn't see the ground properly.*" With the open cockpit he writes of "*often getting frost-bitten.*" Alfred framed many of his engagements as adventures.

After he got good reconnaissance results from flying over the line, General Trenchard, commander of the RFC, commended him. This probably led to his being groomed to fly reconnaissance.

While balloons were often used to spy on enemy troop movements, they proved very vulnerable. Strategists early learned of the importance of coordinating artillery, infantry, airplanes, and the whole panoply of military hardware. Aircraft could track the movements of enemy troops, spot concentrations that might indicate an attack on the line, map enemy fortifications, and assist artillery by spotting the fall of shells.

Without these reconnaissance aircraft, the armies on both sides of the line were basically blind. They had to rely on scouting teams sent into and beyond enemy lines. Planes quickly became essential for artillery spotting, as the batteries could not see their targets or the success of their barrages. Often one plane would be assigned to a particular artillery battery. Communication with the ground was a huge problem. In some cases, messages were dropped by streamers or in packages. Then primitive one-way wireless was installed to transmit simple messages. The wireless machines were too bulky to include both transmission and reception. From 1915 onward, corrections to artillery used Morse code with letters representing distances.

Reconnaissance airplanes held two people, the pilot and the observer who took the pictures and manned the machine gun. My father mentioned several of his observers in his letters.

As the importance of aircraft increased, so did the drive to create innovations to enhance their ability to both fight and observe. These early machines had no radar, which had not been invented, nor many instruments. Gradually better and better cameras were invented so that by the end of the war photographs taken at 15,000 feet could be blown up to show footprints in the mud. As the importance of aerial reconnaissance increased, both the Germans and the British came to depend on photographing the entire front at least twice a day.

Given the danger of flying reconnaissance, it is a wonder that my dad survived. These pilots were not lionized like fighter pilots, but in reality much of the success of the ground war revolved around them. It was extremely dangerous work. As Michael Duffy says at his First World War website, "Because intelligence-gathering aircraft had to fly low and slow along predictable flight paths to photograph the front [with overlapping pictures]…they were often easy victims for enemy fighters and anti-aircraft guns." These pilots seldom survived beyond the average life-span of sixteen weeks.

In order to keep up with developments, Alfred, like other pilots, returned often to Britain for further training. During those periods, he was billeted in the homes of patriotic Brits and Scots. He kept up with many of these families long after the war. During one of those visits he kicked free of military discipline and took his machine for a spin down the Thames. Thereafter he became known as the daredevil who flew under London Bridge. Sadly, I have no confirmation of this feat except hearsay. Later, however, when he was posted back to Canada, he flew under the bridge at Niagara Falls. Papers covered this exploit. To thrive, early pilots had to have a bit of the daredevil in them.

I found no letters between August and December of 1917 to further describe happenings. But Alfred's Christmas letter to his sweetheart indicated that the excitement over flying had dissipated so much that pilots prayed for bad weather so they couldn't fly. The day after Christmas the squadron had a snowball fight!

Sometime in early 1918, Alfred's survival and success led to his being sent back to Canada to train other pilots. He took with him the Croix de Guerre and the Military Cross, awarded for his exploits.

The packet of photos I have from this time in Canada show not only formations and aerial shots of topography but a dozen snaps of crashes. A plane nose-diving into a barracks. Another crashing into a locomotive on the railway. One knocking down a derrick. Planes smashing into the ground upside down. Aircraft crashing into each other. Even one killing a bull in a farmer's field. Clearly, anyone who dared to fly one of these early machines took his life in his hands.

While still on active service, on August 21, 1918, Alfred married Agnes in a ceremony at the Hall farm. They went on to have four sons, of which I am one. Our family is very thankful that Pop survived! A.J. went on to found a trucking company and to build the first parking garage in Montreal. Then came the Depression and he lost it all. But that's another story.

Eric E. Wright's parents Alfred and Agnes Wright

Alfred Wright

Cynthia Reyes

WHEN LIFE GIVES YOU APPLES

If life had given me lemons, perhaps I would have made lemonade. But life gave me apples—a rare, fragrant heritage apple called "Wolf River."

According to apple lore, a French Canadian farmer from Quebec brought some apple seeds to Wolf River, Wisconsin, where he and his family settled in the mid-1800s. Years later, some of the apple seedlings were exported to Canada. A few found their way to an 1860s farm northeast of Toronto, owned by an immigrant family named Glendinning.

The Glendinnings—Thomas and Margaret—had recently arrived from Scotland. They cleared the land, built their farmhouse and barns. The red brick farmhouse was well-built—perhaps a sign of the hope people felt at this auspicious time. The "Fathers of Confederation" were putting together the national framework for the regions that would become Canada in 1867.

Roughly 140 years later, that farmhouse, that history and that apple would become part of the charm that drew our Jamaican-Canadian family to this place.

My husband's family had owned a farm north of Cobourg in Northumberland County. This place reminded us of it, with its sprawling old house, soaring roofline and big, tall trees.

***

The apple trees were the first things we saw when my husband and I turned the corner around the big old house. The two trees were taller than the high farmhouse roof, with a broad spread over the thick green lawn.

"You'll be able to make lots of pies!" I said.

He gave me a big smile.

We were smitten.

***

My body was still whole then—whole and strong—and I immediately pictured myself climbing those trees to pick apples. I'd grown up, yes, but not outgrown this childhood passion. As children in Jamaica, my sisters and I climbed many trees. And when I became an adult in Canada, I saw no reason to stop. I still climbed trees.

"M-o-m!" my daughters had exclaimed when they were younger, half terrified, half-laughing whenever I climbed a tree and disappeared into its leafy branches.

But I never fell, nor even slipped. My heart soared when I climbed a tree, looked down to the ground below and looked above my head, feeling so much closer to the sky. This was happiness.

By the time we moved into the farmhouse, however, climbing trees was the farthest thing from my mind. Some days, I felt as old as the house itself.

I wasn't, of course. At more than 140 years old, the farmhouse had me beat by nearly a century. But our move took place just two weeks after a serious car accident left me badly injured. The injuries cost me my job and a steady income, and left me trapped in the house for weeks, even months, at a time.

What does one do when one is stuck at home, venturing out mainly to visit hospitals, doctors and therapists?

One beautiful fall day, I noticed that the two huge apple trees were festooned with ripening fruit. Did I find myself gazing longingly at the trees, wishing I could climb them? Of course. I stood on the wide veranda and stared and yearned, but I knew the truth: I could no longer climb trees.

Still, life had given us apples—hundreds of apples every other year. So my husband used a long stick to pick the ones closest to the ground, and made apple pies. Big as grapefruit when fully ripe in October, gently sweet and tart at the same time, the Wolf River apple was perfect for cooking.

I had stopped cooking. With a head injury and pain, I couldn't concentrate on the recipes. I'd end up doubling the ingredients, or forgetting some altogether. Some dishes ended up horribly burnt.

My husband finally lost his sense of humour and forbade me from cooking. He took over almost all the cooking and baking. He was right, of course. But I felt even more useless.

***

What to do with all those apples? I wondered as I stared at the still hundreds of reddening fruit on the tree.

After my husband had made a dozen apple pies?

After we had given large bags of fruit to neighbours, relatives, friends and even strangers?

Ah...Apple jelly! I suddenly remembered apple jelly.

I used to make delicious apple and herb jellies. Perhaps I could do it again?

"Of course not," came the doubting voice in my head. I knew this voice well; it had become the resident sound track to my life.

But now I shook my head to clear it of doubt.

"It's worth a try," I told myself.

Jars of jelly, I thought—made from our rare Wolf River apples—would make inexpensive and thoughtful Christmas presents for relatives and close friends. I no longer earned my own money, and we were living frugally.

***

Maneuvering with my good arm, assisted weakly by the other, I set to work quartering the apples, then boiling them in a large pot on the stove of our traditional farmhouse kitchen. I was committed. I was going to do this.

"What on earth are you doing?" my husband asked as he walked into the kitchen. He saw the look of pure determination on my face. Perhaps he also realized the task would take me forever. He quickly decided to help.

From his herb garden my good man brought me the mint I needed. From the grocery store he brought me cheesecloth for straining the cooked mixture, and bags of sugar to help thicken the liquid.

He left me on my own to monitor the boiling liquid in the huge pot. I watched and waited to make sure the liquid jelled.

Making jelly is a simple task for some people. Not me. I ruined whole batches at first. I failed to let the mixture boil long enough and it didn't jell sufficiently. Then I made the mistake of adding more cups of sugar, which made the jelly entirely too sweet.

Another time I stepped away briefly and the boiling liquid frothed up and over the rim of the pot, making a sticky mess of stove, countertop and floor.

But, still determined, I returned the next day and the next, staying with it until I got it right.

"Hmmm…" my husband said whenever he came into the kitchen. Then: "Mmm-hmmm."

The sweet-spicy scent of apple and mint jelly filled the kitchen for days on end.

Together we strained the hot apple mixture through the cheesecloth, measured out the sugar to pour into the pot while stirring, boiled the jars to sterilize them and, finally, poured the hot jelly into the jars.

One afternoon, after we had filled and sealed nearly eighty jars of jelly, he walked into the kitchen and handed me several thick sheets of labels.

"I made these for you," he said.

Each label bore a picture of our farmhouse. The beautiful Ontario farmhouse that was almost as old as Canada's Confederation. The picture on the label—taken by my husband—captured the dark red brick, soaring roofline, wide verandas and mullioned windows.

I stared at my labels, then into my husband's smiling face, and laughed. It was hard to figure out who was prouder.

Gwynn Scheltema

NAARTJIES

Outside my window
my garden declares itself a Tom Thomson painting.
Blue spruce hangs heavy
each branch white-gloved
square-fingered
tree shadows dance purple on snow.
Barely dawn, a pale orange sky backlights the birch
a swaying golden head in early morning light.
I hold up a clementine to the pane
and picture it as the sun.

This clementine skin is thin,
clings fast.
It has travelled a long way,
is old.
When I was a child
a clementine tree grew outside my window
—*naartjies* we called them
over there
in Zimbabwe.

In November, when the rains finally broke
great clouds pregnant with water
released upon the earth
The world became mud;
people, cars, and streets were awash with it

frogs bubbled from its depths.
Yet—beyond my window,
through glasswater
just visible
the orange *naartjie* suns.

Today the air is tight with cold.
I dress in layers, zip on my boots,
take up a bucket of kitchen scraps to empty in the compost.

Snow squeaks in protest,
its surface forever scarred by my passing.
I sweep the black composter with mitted hand;
the snow is dry. It's that cold.
I lift the lid, toss in *naartjie* skins, watch them fall,
so far from their roots, their beginnings,
no longer young, basking under an African sun, welcoming the
rain.

They have journeyed across the ocean
drawn their skins tight about them in this cold north.
They have sustained and nourished,
resting now on the compost pile
knowing that there were moments when
they were the sun.

Katie Hoogendam

GARDENING

When I came to Canada,
I left Michigan behind.
I left my parents behind,
my sisters behind; the big red house,
the old record player, encased in mahogany,
the driveway made of sand, dune grass,
the Coho salmon, the Homestead Dam,
Crystal Lake, the family cemetery,
the overstuffed leather chair ripped stem to stern by a rotating
cast of cats,
all of it, behind.

But it seems despair came with me,
snuck into the bright red hard-sided suitcase I bought
at Adana's yard sale for three bucks.
And fear, she came too, wrapped up in tissue paper
as if fragile (a disguise).
I wanted hope to come, effervescence,
but it turns out they had other plans.

Instead I was left
with three anonymous seeds,
different sizes.
Somehow these seeds made the trip unmolested.
Unpacking in Ontario, I was surprised to find them.
I'm no gardener, but then again, I'm not sure what I am.

It seemed strange, these three seeds on the bedside table at two
in the morning.
Some things need to be in the ground.

I got out of bed and with a trowel in my hand, dug a hole.
It was dark, but it turns out the moon
is the same cross border.
I put all three seeds in one hole,
spaced apart an inch or so. I was afraid
I'd forget about them, but I didn't.
I watered them and waited.
It seemed to take forever.

One morning, bright with dew on the spiderwebs
across the porch rail, I saw it—
one green shoot.
The place was a rental so I had to leave before the main event.
I never learned the phrenology
of the botanicals,
but I saw what happens when you tend a thing

Erika Rummel

THE NEWCOMER

I thought it would be harder to find a place to live as a newcomer. In Detroit nobody rents anything to you after you come out of the slammer, except maybe a mattress in a flophouse. But Julian said Canadians are easygoing. He gave me a phone number to call in Toronto. Old Bev will rent you a place, he said. Just keep your fingers from her stuff. Okay, I said, although I didn't see why that should worry him.

The old woman rented me a room, no questions asked. *And* it's a posh neighbourhood. They have dog walkers here. And landscapers, who pick dandelions out of the lawn by hand. That's the kind of neighbourhood it is. My room isn't posh, though. It's in the basement and crammed with old-people furniture. There's a closet-sized bathroom and a fridge and microwave in the common laundry area. It's okay, except that the room has no door. It's open concept. It used to be the rec room, Bev said. So now she can pad downstairs any time she wants, pretending to do the laundry and checking up on me instead. I'll have to do something about that, but what? On the other hand, there is no way *she* can secure her place either. The whole first floor is open concept. I've been through everything, including the bedrooms on the second floor and the third-floor studio, or whatever it is, a strange empty space with a futon on the floor and mysterious cut-outs dangling from the slanted walls: moons and stars and the logo from the old TV show *Charmed.* None of her rooms are locked. I guess old Bev is the trusting kind. That's how they are here, Julian said. Too trusting for their own good.

Bev is seventy-eight years old and looking her age. There are liver spots on the backs of her hands, and her face is sagging badly, especially around the eyes and mouth, and the lipstick (she always wears lipstick) bleeds into the little lines radiating off her lips. She dresses smartly, but she walks in that careful, deliberate way old people have. She still has all her marbles, though. That's why I can't believe how careless she was. She took me in without running a background check. I just mentioned Julian's name and said I was a student.

"That's nice," she said. "What are you studying, Tracy?"

"English literature," I said. I thought she might like that.

She did.

"Oh, my favourite subject," she said.

And that was that. I handed over first and last month's rent and moved my bags into the basement.

I waited until I had her schedule figured out. She goes to the hairdresser on Friday afternoons. Tuesday and Thursday evenings she gets together with three old biddies to play bridge. She does her shopping in the morning. I can be reasonably sure of having the house to myself between 10 and 12 a.m. She leaves money lying around—three twenties and change, on the kitchen counter. I took one of the twenties. To hell with my promise to Julian. I figured I could get away with that much. Next morning, she came downstairs. I thought she was going to question me, but she just wanted help with her cell phone, how to set the alarm. I showed her and noticed the brown spots on her hands were lighter. Is there some cream on the market to bleach liver spots?

The next time she was out playing bridge, I looked around. Her jewellery was all over the place, but I took only a pair of small gold earrings she left beside the TV. They fetched a reasonable price at the pawnbroker's. It was a good week for me. I went to the Reference Library and made off with a laptop. People are so careless here. It was a bit risky, mind you. Lots of people milling around, but I got away with it. I'm good at that: becoming invisible, blending in with the crowd, fading away. Julian usually buys the electronic stuff from me.

He has a chaotic shop on Queen Street. There is a piece of cardboard taped to the door that says "Electronic equipment bought, sold, repaired." The rest you have to read between the lines. Inside are shelves and shelves of electronic equipment, whole or in parts, a tangled mess illuminated by a single 60-watt bulb. Julian doesn't need much light for his business. He doesn't even need the computers, but he loves fooling around with them, hacking into bank accounts and private emails, that sort of thing. Plus, the computers form a kind of protective rampart behind which he conducts his other business. Julian's face is camouflaged with a giant beard and wild hair. From time to time he mows his face for no discernible reason and emerges pale-skinned and blue-eyed, but most of the time his face is a shaggy carpet. In spite of his sedentary job, Julian is a hunk. And he has a great coiling dragon tattoo in the small of his back, where his T-shirt fails to meet his pants. In fact, I have a crush on Julian, but I'm just a stray cat to him.

So after I sold him the laptop, I was flush. For two days I didn't go upstairs except once, and then I only took one of Bev's bras, as a joke, because it was such an antediluvian contraption, white, with clasps in front like a nursing bra, padded cups shaped like cones, wide straps. I put it on and took a couple of pics of myself in Bev costume, to post on Facebook for Halloween. Or not. You never know who's looking at your wall. But it would have been a nice revenge. She pissed me off the other day when she said, "Tracy, don't put KFC boxes into the blue bin. They should go into the regular garbage, dear."

"You know what?" I said to Julian. "I'm tired of Canadians already. They are so fucking law-and-order. What's with the recycling mania? And picking up dog shit with their hands sheathed in little plastic bags? And painting over graffiti so fast it barely has time to dry?"

Bev raised her voice when she said "Put the KFC boxes into the blue bin." She was angry because she had told me once before, but really, she should thank me for raising her pulse rate. She looked good. The anger lifted her face and improved the colour of her cheeks. Well, maybe there's more to her improved looks than a raised pulse rate. Maybe she's latched on to Botox and fillers. She can afford the treatments. Anyway, I got my revenge: I went through the drawers in her bedroom and found a list with passwords and PIN numbers. Now I just have to find the matching cards, but that's one area in which the old woman is careful. She doesn't leave her credit cards lying around, and she hangs on to her purse at all times.

Every time she goes out, I nip upstairs and look around, but no cards. She has converted one of the bedrooms into an "office." I don't know what she needs an office for. To keep the bridge scores? I turn on her ancient computer, but I get sidetracked by a brooch that's lying on the desk. It's antique, and I take it against my better judgment. I don't get much for it at the pawnbroker's, and it's high risk, easily identified. For a few days I walk in fear, but Bev says nothing. Maybe her brain is deteriorating while her appearance is improving. I notice the creases around her mouth are smoothing out. She is definitely getting filler injected there.

Bazinga! One of the numbers on the list is the combination for her wall safe. It contains mostly papers: her birth certificate, her will (Bev's money goes to the Humane Society), the deed for the house, a bundle of letters, and in a box, half a dozen Krugerrands—six ounces of gold! That was easy. I wish I could hang on to them because the price of gold is rising. But I like the feel of cash. It's untraceable. Julian takes the coins off my hands. I get home with a nice stash, but I can't enjoy it as much as I normally would because

I'm feeling under the weather. Sore, creaky. I think I'm coming down with something. I look dreadful. Grey and beagle-eyed.

Three days later. Still no improvement. On the contrary, I feel a hundred years old. Bev comes skipping down the stairs. "Can I do anything for you, Tracy?" she chirps. I want to say, Go away, but all I can muster is a groan. She leaves me a bottle of multivitamins and bounds back upstairs. I swear she's enjoying herself. She likes seeing me on my back. It makes her feel better by contrast.

When I hear her drive off to do the shopping, I drag myself upstairs and am rewarded for the effort: Bev has left her computer on. A website is up, a Wicca site. Who would have thought Bev was interested in witchcraft? I decide to check her personal files. Some of the file names look intriguing, but I don't get around to opening them because I see that Bev has left her Visa card beside the computer. She must have ordered something from the Wicca site. What, I wonder? Anyway: this is my lucky day. It's a platinum card. But I have to force myself to take it, I don't know why. It must be the flu. I pocket the card, get my coat on, trudge to the nearest ATM and start punching in the PIN numbers I have for Bev. The second one works. I take out an inconspicuous sum: $120. And I have to talk myself into pocketing that much. It's not just caution. Something is holding me back. Bad conscience? Naw, couldn't be. A distaste for stealing? I must be really sick.

I schlep home and put the credit card back where I found it, on the desk beside the computer. I briefly consider looking into Bev's files, but I'm too tired. I'm bushwhacked. I think I'll go to the walk-in clinic for a checkup.

I go downstairs to get my health card. I reach for my wallet. It's not where I left it. I look everywhere, but I can't find it. I mean it's not exactly small, it's the size of a clutch purse, but it's gone. This is too much. I collapse on the sofa. I'll deal with this later.

At noon, I hear Bev's car pull into the driveway. She comes into the house and tramps downstairs.

"Tracy?" she calls. "Tracy? Are you there, dear?"

"I'm here," I say. My voice has gone quavery, like an old woman's.

She comes right into my room and steps up to the sofa where I'm lying, bushed. She looks vibrant.

"Poor thing," she says, and puts her hand on my forehead. "You're not running a fever, are you? No, it feels okay," she says and withdraws her hand. I notice it's nice and plump. The liver spots are gone. I close my eyes.

"Something embarrassing happened to me yesterday," she says, and when I open my eyes again, she is holding up my wallet.

"I took this by mistake," she says. "I don't know how it happened—I'm so sorry, Tracy," she says, but she doesn't look it.

I study her face. I haven't noticed it before, but she looks a bit like me, like a crook. Wouldn't that be something if she was a thief, too? Well, she won't get anything from me. I keep the cash in my pocket and spend it as fast as I can. And I have nothing else she'd want.

The flu, or whatever it was, went away just as quickly as it had come. The fever broke at night—I had a violent dream, a poltergeist kind of dream with noise going on upstairs, people walking back and forth, arguing in repressed tones, then silence. And in the morning I woke up feeling good.

Around ten, Bev goes off to do her shopping, but a little later I hear steps overhead. No, I must be mistaken, I think. Is the flu back? Am I having hallucinations? I hear someone coming down the stairs and turning into the laundry area. I've tacked up a blanket over my non-existent door, over the opening into the hallway—a privacy curtain. That means I can't see who/what is coming down the stairs, and I can't tell: Am I dreaming? Or is Bev back already? I can't stand it. I have to check. I go out into the hall. The light in the laundry area is on. There is someone in there loading the washing machine. A man.

He stops what he is doing and looks up. Even with his beard and hair neatly trimmed, I recognize his messianic presence at once. It's Julian, tall, lanky, giving me his magnetic blue-eyed stare, macho in spite of the domestic chore of pushing dirty clothes into the washer.

"Julian!" I say. "What are you doing here?

"Fucking landlord locked me out. Had the place declared a safety hazard," he says with his usual mixture of hot charm and profanity. "The inspector came in and found a couple of baggies, you know what I mean? I'm up next week."

That explains his clean-cut looks. In prep for the court appearance the blond mane and the scraggly beard had to go. But it doesn't explain how he got into the house.

"How did you get in?"

"I have a key."

"I didn't know you were such good friends, you and Bev."

"She's my mother," he says.

"No!" I say.

"Yes!" he says. "Well, sort of."

What the hell does "sort of" mean?

He puts on his believe-it-or-not voice and tells me a story.

He was born at St. Mike's Hospital, he says, when Bev was there for a hysterectomy. That's twenty-eight years ago. When it was time for her to go home, she took him along. Kidnapped baby Julian and kept him in the attic for three months until the police tracked him down. Not that Julian's mother was desperate to find her baby. She was a prostitute on crack, but the Children's Aid Society kept the case going, and so Julian was found. Bev got off lightly because a psychiatrist testified on her behalf. He said she was clinically depressed, distraught after the hysterectomy, which signified the end of her womanhood, and so she went temporarily insane and took the baby. No harm had come to the child, he pointed out. In fact Bev had doted on him. The doctor who conducted the medical examination confirmed that the child was in excellent health, but noted two pin pricks, as if someone had poked Julian's arm with a needle. The marks were never explained. Bev got off with a slap on the wrist: a hundred hours of community service and obligatory attendance in a counselling program.

Julian ended up in a series of foster homes. When he was sixteen, he went to see Bev. He rang her doorbell. She came out, eyed him, and said: "There you are!" He lived with her for the next two years.

"But life with Bev comes at a price," he said to me. "You pay for everything you get."

"What do you mean?"

"She's a witch. She takes it out of you. Those mysterious pinpricks they found on my arms when I was a baby? She sucked my blood."

I had never heard Julian talk crap like that. He isn't the superstitious kind.

"Come on, Julian," I said. "That's crazy."

"You think so? Then how do you explain that she and I have the same DNA?" He had tests done, he said. He could prove it. "But when I confronted Bev with the results, she laughed and said, 'Well, that explains why I took you home with me.' That's all I managed to get out of her."

It was too weird. I changed the topic. "So how long are you planning to stay?"

"Couple of weeks. Bev put me up on the top floor."

"In the studio with the mobiles and a futon on the floor?"

"You've been scoping out the place. Snagged a few of her things?"

I shrugged my shoulders.

"Don't. Didn't I warn you? She'll take something from you in exchange."

"I don't have anything she'd want."

"That's what you think!" he said. "You do have something: youth."

I laughed in his face. "Yeah, sure. And she's going to take that from me?" But when I look into the mirror, I'm no longer certain. Was there a tit-for-tat spell? You eat my food, baby, and I take your pristine blood? You take my money, Tracy, and I take your looks?

Okay, so I said to Julian I wouldn't take any more of Bev's stuff, but that doesn't include looking at her computer files. I have so many questions about her now. Maybe the answers are in the files.

One morning, when I'm alone in the house, I go upstairs and turn on Bev's computer. And you know what? The C-drive has been wiped. There isn't a single file there. Julian must have worked on the machine and pitted his tech magic against Bev's Wicca spells. I go out into the hall and look up to the third-floor landing. I see that Julian has put a lock on the studio door and taped up a piece of paper with an eye painted on it, one of those King Tut eyes, almond-shaped, black-rimmed, and unflinching. I guess that means we are safe from Bev for the time being, Julian and I.

Shane Joseph

GROWING UP IN TORONTO

JIMMY

My parents were teachers in Scarborough in the seventies, before that city was swept up into the megacity of Toronto. We led an ordered life: school, homework, household chores, mass on Sunday; the annual summer trip to Algonquin Park or cottage country, regular attendance at the community theatre and, perhaps once a year, a splurge at a choral concert downtown. Mom and Dad communicated via ritual tasks. When she silently placed his dinner before him at 7 p.m. sharp, he would shift his newspaper, glance at his plate and nod contentedly. If the plate arrived any time after the seventh gong had sounded on the hall clock, he would spend the rest of that evening pacing the living room, puffing on his pipe. Likewise, if he did not arrive with the groceries at exactly 6:30 p.m. each Wednesday evening, she would pull out her rosary and pray by the window.

George Walton's home, by contrast, was organized bedlam. His father, the supreme commander, ran a construction business when he was not a provincial member of parliament. Their house was a parade of builders, constituents, realtors, engineers, business people and other denizens coming and going at all hours. George's overworked mother rushed back and forth replenishing tea, cookies and other refreshments for all who came. Her husband did not give her any respite, bellowing for more tea or for the bottle of Scotch to appease his elusive flock. As a teenager growing up in Scarborough, I was drawn to the Walton home, if only to escape the sterility of mine.

George was full of grandiose plans even then. He hated his father's shouting at his mother—I didn't know how much until we met the raccoon—yet admired the elder Walton's business and political savvy. George's ambition was to be better than his father. He was going to be prime minister of Canada when he grew up—a powerful magnet for someone like me looking for a role model.

One summer's day, during the school break, I went to George's as we had arranged to go to the park to fly our kites. Mr. Walton answered my knock on the front door. He was busy talking to a man in a business suit. Mr. Walton scarcely paid me any notice other than to hold the door open and say, "George is busy. Come in, but don't disturb him." I nodded and headed for George's bedroom and found my friend at his desk.

"What's happened?" I asked in dismay.

"I can't go. Dad won't let me, until I finish my homework."

"Homework during holidays?"

"Dad says I've got to brush up on trigonometry, because it's part of next year's program. 'Got to keep the mind active, my boy!'"

"But it must be hard. We've not even read up on it yet."

"It's easy, just a bunch of silly calculations. And it's done. I've figured it out."

"You have? You're a genius!"

"Piece of cake."

"So, if you are done, what's the problem?"

"Dad wants me to spend two hours on this assignment—that's how long he thinks it will take to 'do it justice,' as he says."

"He doesn't know you're smarter than that?"

"He doesn't know much. But I've got a plan. When that man in the suit dropped by, I slipped into Dad's study and moved the clock forward by half an hour. He's going back into his study when he sees the man off. Go around the back and wait for me."

I took the kites and went around the back of the house. I paused by the open study window and peeked in. Mr. Walton had returned and was smoking at his desk, deeply engrossed in what looked like building diagrams. George entered.

"Here you are. It's done," he said in a flat voice.

"Humph." His father did not even look up.

"It's done, Dad."

Mr. Walton looked up this time, not at his son, but at the clock. "Hmm. Five o'clock. About time. Leave it there. I'll correct it when I am done." George turned on his heel and walked away rapidly.

Within seconds he was grabbing my arm in the garden and pulling me. "Run!"

Only when we were a few yards down the driveway did the neighbourhood church ring its bell announcing the half hour—4:30 p.m. I'm glad they outlawed church bells soon after that. George never told me how much his father beat him for that offence, but he sported a noticeable limp for a few days afterwards.

***

Later that summer, we went raccoon hunting. George's house overlooked Birkdale Ravine, and during warmer weather raccoons crept up the hill and attacked the garbage. His mother was constantly swearing at the trails of smelly chicken bones strewn around that she had to clean up before George's father's constituents came by. Sometimes she didn't make it in time and Walton Sr. would become incensed and yell at her, and George would hold his ears and grimace.

When I went over to his place that day, George was in the backyard carving a V-shaped stick from a pile of freshly broken branches off the giant maple. Thick rubber bands and leather patches cut off an old shoe lay on the ground beside him.

"Slingshot," he explained when I enquired.

I sat on the stoop and watched. When he was finished, George checked the weapon's aim by placing a pebble in the leather sling, closing and gripping it firmly in his hand, then pulling back on the rubber bands and releasing the stone, through the V, at a tin can twenty feet away. He hit the can on the third try.

"It's swinging left. Here, you can have this one." He tossed the faulty slingshot at me and picked up another V-shaped branch. "The next one will be perfect."

Two hours later, we were armed with a slingshot each.

"Come on, let's go hunt those bastards."

But raccoons are never around when you want them. We scoured the ravine in the midday heat along the banks of the creek, which was stagnant in patches. George practised by taking trial shots at dogs out for exercise, while their owners talked to each other and momentarily took their eyes off their pets. When the animals yelped and ran like their world was ending, the owners were jerked out of their chatting to embrace the consequences of their negligence, and two eleven-year-old boys stumbled through the bushes, sometimes falling into mud on the soft banks of the creek, running just as fast as the dogs—in the opposite direction.

"Maybe we'll find raccoons only in the early morning or late in the evening," I said. "They must be asleep now." I was panting from our last getaway and rapidly tiring of the raccoon hunt, or the chase, if indeed those pet owners were closing on our tails at that moment.

But George paid no heed, and we continued to spend the next two hours looking for our prey. At our last stop, he made me hide behind some bushes along the smelliest part of the creek, where a big blob of rapidly decomposing fruit had lodged against an overhanging branch dipping into the water. The smell began to make me puke.

George had remained highly agitated throughout the hunt and there was fire in his eyes. "They've gotta come here. That smell's the same as in our garbage cans."

And then we heard the shaking of branches and the clumsy amble of the scavenger: a full-sized raccoon, as big as a dog, making its way down the bank on the other side, stopping occasionally to ferret out scraps inside empty wrappers and used Styrofoam containers.

I'd wished that son-of-a-bitch raccoon had come five minutes earlier. The sickly-sweet smell of the degenerating fruit and the sight of that waddling grey fur-ball adding its own stench to the scene took me over the edge.

I retched loudly.

The animal pricked up its ears and started backing up the hill. George broke cover, aiming his slingshot and letting fly, but the animal was moving faster and I lost sight of what happened next because I was throwing up into the bushes around me.

"Sorry," I offered and retched again. But George was gone in a crash of branches and a splash of water as he ran across the shallow creek, yelling, "Come back, you bastard. Come back and die!"

When I had emptied my stomach sufficiently and crawled up the bank, out of smell-shot of the rotting fruit, I heard him returning, swearing under his breath.

"Son-of-a-bitch, why did you have to do that?"

"I told you, I was getting sick the minute we got there. Did you get him?"

I thought he was going to shoot me next, he looked so mad.

"No. But I'll get him tomorrow."

***

GEORGE

The next morning George went out alone. He was waiting behind the tool shed at five o'clock. The birds had started chirping a few minutes earlier and awoken him. His parents were still asleep; their laboured snores followed him as he tiptoed out the back door. He had to keep Jimmy out of this—the poor loser only got in the way.

He breathed in the cool air; dew covered the tree line that stretched downhill into the ravine. The tool shed was just at the drop-off point—easy access to scavengers coming out of the creek below. This property was his home; no one—animal or human—was going to take it away from him. And nothing should upset the balance of his parents' fragile relationship, strained as it had been these last few years since his father had entered politics.

His mother's tired looks at the end of a day of frenzied activity around the house, his father drinking his daily Scotch, elevated to a double now, the shouting matches that lapsed into loud silences—yes, things had definitely changed at home, for the worse. Sometimes he wondered if his father cared for his mother anymore, or was she just a servant now?

His frustration started to gain focus as he narrowed his sights on the animal scurrying up the hill in the half-light, moving toward the shed.

The stones weighed heavy in his pocket, carefully selected for weight and balance after he had returned from his fruitless quest with Jimmy the day before. Now, he aimed at the centre of the ambling shadow.

The first stone stunned the creature. It froze, then deflated. The second stone must have hurt for it elicited a faint bleat-like sound. George left the shelter of the shed and advanced on his quarry, third stone drawn. A second four-legged shadow was hurrying up the hill—enemy reinforcements. George stayed with the fallen one; *hit them where they are weakest, do not fight on many fronts,* lessons from the books he had read on WWII military strategy. The third stone hit the wounded animal with a flat *thunk* and sent its companion scurrying down the hill where branches around the creek flittered in a diminishing wave, whisking away the second animal.

George paused and waited for his target to move again. It started limping, slowly. He followed it. It paused by the shed. A plank had been placed leaning against the roof at a forty-five degree angle; the animal started to advance along it. *Good! Just where I want you.*

He waited until the raccoon was at roof level and fired the fourth stone. With a cry, almost human, the creature rolled over onto the roof, marooned now, unable to descend until its attacker relented.

Daylight was breaking rapidly. George climbed the tall maple tree next to the shed, the bag of stones banging against his thigh. He was at eye level with the creature now, four feet away, foxy face, fear written everywhere, even in the foul smell emanating from it.

"Don't mess with my family, you bastard," George said and shot the fifth stone. He saw the blood spurt this time, from the mouth, splashing the shed's roof.

He heard footsteps below.

Jimmy!

"What the heck are you doing up here so early?" George hissed.

Jimmy was in his pyjamas; he looked like he had left his house down the road in a hurry. "I had a dream that you were hunting raccoons again."

"I thought you'd had enough yesterday."

"Yes, but something bad was happening in this dream. I came to warn you." Jimmy was agitated and insistent.

That was when the raccoon made a desperate attempt to escape and leapt off the roof, hit the plank, couldn't hold on, and fell with a thud onto an upward-looking Jimmy.

Animal and boy went down in a heap. Animal and human squealing coalesced and George couldn't make out one from the other. In their bid to be free of each other, they seemed to have locked tighter together. George let off another stone at the soft brown furry side of the struggling animal-boy. He missed, and Jimmy screamed in agony. The shot helped dislodge the pair, however, and the raccoon limped away before rolling downhill and crashing into the underbrush below.

George jumped down from the maple and went to his friend's assistance. Jimmy had scratch marks on his face and his clothes were torn, a red welt forming on his forehead.

"You shouldn't have come," George said. Jimmy had slipped into a bout of shivering. "I had the whole thing under control."

"George! What the hell's going on?" Walton Sr. was on the back deck and advancing, a dressing gown hastily thrown over his nightclothes. George's mother peeked from behind a curtain, a look of shock on her face. She was already sucking hard on her first cigarette of the day.

"It was the raccoon," George said. But that did not prevent the slap that his father gave him.

"We…we weren't fighting, Mr. Walton," Jimmy added weakly.

George saw his mother enter the yard, clothed only in her nightdress. Taking in a deep breath, she threw away her half-smoked cigarette and ran to his fallen friend's assistance. He'd never seen such decisiveness in her in his father's presence.

"It was the raccoon," George insisted. "I shot the raccoon!"

His father had him by the ear and was hauling George indoors.

"Leave him be," his mother wailed while cradling Jimmy's head in her lap.

"Shut up, woman. Get that kid indoors. And yourself too. You look like a tart in that nightie." Walton Sr. swung another blow at

George's head. "And you. . .you're grounded, you dumbass. What will the neighbours think of us?"

George wrenched himself free of his father's grip and felt something explode in his eardrum. His father looked incredulously at his empty fingers. Through the pounding pain George ran across the yard to the deck, jumped on it, and looked down at his father. "*I* shot the raccoon. *I* am the victor and *you* are the dumbass. *You* are the raccoon. I shot him so you wouldn't shout at Mom anymore."

Patricia Calder

RIPPLES ON A POND

I was born in Stratford, Ontario, as was my father. His father built a house on Water Street, three blocks from what is now the Stratford Festival Theatre. Every day after four o'clock, as a boy, my dad would walk home from Juliet Public School past his grandfather's house, also on Water Street. His grandfather was a pioneer, instrumental in providing Stratford with pure water from artesian wells. In that same public school, in the same classroom as my father, sat another boy, one who would become famous—Tom Patterson, key founder of the Stratford Festival, in honour of whom one of the festival's four theatres is named.

On a recent visit to the famous Festival Theatre, I parked outside my grandfather's former house on Water Street and knocked on the door. The couple who now own the house are both doctors, with four small children. When I showed them pictures of their home as it was being built by my grandfather, they invited me in and showed me through the house. I was able to introduce them to a laundry chute they didn't know existed, and tell them about the "Bird Room," where my grandfather kept his collection of canaries. Occasionally he would let one or two out of their cages to fly around the house.

Houses hold memories. Visiting the house that my father grew up in and where I spent the first year of my life brought back memories of childhood visits to Stratford when my grandparents were still alive. Walking beside the Avon River brought to memory a story my father had told me. He once rode the ice floes in spring, wearing new shoes and britches with long socks over his long underwear. He fell in, soaking his new shoes, thus earning a licking when he went home. As a teen, he played tennis most days with his cousin and best friend, Barron, whom, a few short years later, he witnessed being killed in WWII.

My father and mother met as children at Inverhuron Beach, where both their families rented cottages year after year. When my dad came home during the war, he visited his sister's new baby and he ran into my mother, who worked as a nurse in that maternity wing. She refused to go out with him because he had been a brat as a child, so she arranged several dates with other nurses for him. Finally, she agreed to one date, just bowling.

My mother had four brothers. Phillip was wounded with shrapnel in Italy. He became a foreign correspondent with CBC, reporting on the erection of the Berlin Wall years later. Jack became a sportswriter for the *Toronto Telegram*. When WWII started, he joined the Air Force, lost his bearings in fog and landed in neutral Ireland, which was taking prisoners from both sides. Jack was captured and taken to the notorious Eire prison. He wrote furiously, stories he called "The Boys at the Front." When his older brother visited he would smuggle out the stories and send them home, where they hit major newspapers across Canada. My grandmother kept a scrapbook of them that I now treasure. Jack escaped twice, only to be shot down over Germany in the last year of the war.

Jake became a famous alcoholic. I say famous because he travelled with AA giving speeches at meetings across North America, and the Calder Rehabilitation Centre in Saskatchewan was named after him. When he hit bottom again, he was rescued by his younger brother, Phillip, brought to Toronto, dressed in a new suit, and introduced at City Hall. Soon he developed a second career as a writer for politicians. His gift of the gab paid off again. Unfortunately, tragedy followed Jake around. First, his wife committed suicide, then one of his children, then one of his grandchildren.

Suicide has been a ripple in the pond of my mother's family. Her other brother, Gerald, died in a shooting gallery in Montreal, a suspected suicide. I grew up with the myth that my mother had lost two brothers during the war, Jack and Gerald. I believed that Gerald had also been shot overseas until I was twelve and we moved to Montreal. I overheard my parents quarrelling in the kitchen. Mother wanted to contact the police to find out what really happened to Gerald. Father said, "Don't dig up the past."

My mother's grandfather came from Scotland to settle on Campobello Island, New Brunswick, where he married one of three sisters and became a sea captain. All three sisters married and lived in large houses on the same bluff overlooking the ocean. My great-grandfather Calder soon owned a fleet of fishing vessels and opened the first canning factory on the east coast. He had four sons, one of whom, my great-uncle Franklin, taught Franklin Delano Roosevelt and his brothers how to sail. The Roosevelts had a summer home on Campobello and spent many vacations there.

In 1921 when FDR was diagnosed with polio on Campobello, Uncle Franklin and five sturdy islanders carried him on a stretcher down the long winding path to the water and transported him along the coast by motorboat. Then they lifted him onto a luggage wagon, thence through the window of a train bound for Presbyterian Hospital, New York. Eleanor Roosevelt gave Captain Calder an engraved watch as a thank-you gift. Thereafter, on FDR's subsequent trips to Campobello, Captain Calder would be summoned to prepare the boat.

The Calder spawn spread out over the Maritimes and from there all over Canada and the US until today there are hundreds if not thousands of Calders. Shops, businesses, streets, a town, an arena, even two cemeteries were all named after the Calders. Hockey players, doctors, lawyers and criminals, they drifted into all walks of life. My grandfather was first a lawyer, then an Anglican minister, and finally an MPP for Chatham-Kent district, and minister of education. He could regularly be seen walking home from the Saturday market with a live chicken dangling from his fist.

After my divorce, when I changed my name to Calder, my mother's maiden name, my father was a bit hurt. I explained that I did not choose his name (Mason), not to dishonour him, but to honour my mother. About this time a story emerged that soothed his wounded ego. As it turns out, my father's real name was not Mason either, but Meredith. Generations before, a young man, John Meredith, in England, fell in love with an illiterate Irish woman named Anna. She had lovely brown eyes but she was beneath his station and four years his senior. He was not permitted to marry her, even though she was six months pregnant with his child. When his father discovered how his son had disgraced the family name, he was thrown out of the house. He had, after all, sung in the choir of Westminster Abbey and studied for the ministry. He, and Anna, came to Canada instead, and he changed his name from John Meredith to Mason, his mother's maiden name. Today, three generations of Masons have been anchored in Canada, and so a fiction has become reality.

At the age of eighteen I fell in love with Prince Edward Island. I felt the ocean, ancestral voices, calling my name. Finally at the age of forty, I bought an acre of land overlooking the blue, blue horizon and built a house. My father had practised flying out of Summerside airport before he was sent overseas on a ship from Halifax. He gave me his navigational maps. What a connection that was. I had thought he hated me, or I hated him, one or the other.

When I retired, I searched for a house with a view of the water. After I moved to Colborne, Ontario, a cousin informed me that our great-grandparents were buried in the Salem cemetery, just down the road. We visited the church and located the gravestones. They were my father's mother's parents, whose names I had never known. They married in Colborne and lived the rest of their lives on Church Street, one block from where I now live.

Ripples on a pond move out in circles, but they also ripple back, and keep reverberating.

Sharon Ramsey Curtis

THE BIRTH OF A SHOPPER

In the spring of 1977, I was raising my children in a small town in Ontario, Canada. Looking back, I realize that life was much simpler then. It was safe: we even expected that children would go exploring beyond parental eyesight. Adventuring away from the confines of home was part of growing up and moving out into the world. It was a rite of passage for our growing children.

Around this time, yard sales had become all the rage. Like mushrooms after a spring rain, lawns, patios, and driveways bristled with all kinds of useful items. There were baskets, rowing machines, ice cream makers, and rusty hibachis. There were partial sets of silverware, barely used pots and pans, and knives that had potential to turn you immediately into a first-class chef. Buttons, zippers, and fabric were available in a staggering array of colours. Certainly, the odd antique could be found if you had a discerning eye.

One Saturday in early May my four-year-old daughter was making the rounds of the neighbours' sales and I was puttering in the garden.

Suddenly she came running breathlessly from her morning adventures. She was full of the wonders that she had seen. It was an early indication to me that she was headed toward life as an enthusiastic shopper.

At that moment there was one thing, and one thing only, that beckoned to her. She believed that she was likely to expire if she did not purchase it immediately. She just needed fifty cents for this most amazing thing! With no clue as to her heart's desire I handed over fifty cents and off she hurried. I remember thinking, *How much trouble could she buy with such a small amount of money?*

A long time elapsed. I began to wonder what could be keeping her. I peered up and down the street and could see, in the distance, a slow procession moving my way. It appeared to have no human shape; I became quite curious. As the shape drew closer it began to morph in front of my eyes. It became a small and very spindly daughter who hauled upon her back a very large purple frog. It was hilariously amusing, with wobbly eyes and a huge green-and-gold-checkered belly. My enthusiastic shopper fizzed with unalloyed joy, her happiness complete.

She has it to this day, and in retrospect, I consider it a gift from the universe that my fifty cents did not buy anything that required walking, feeding, or visits to the vet.

It was a narrow escape!

Linda Hutsell Manning

THE FRONT ROAD SCHOOL WEST: A NEW BEGINNING

On a hot day early in July 1963, I sit nervously on a straight-backed chair in a narrow, airless foyer of the Cold Springs Memorial Hall. I'm waiting to be interviewed for a Hamilton Township teaching position in a one-room school between Cobourg and Port Hope. Two Cobourg Town School interviews have been unsuccessful mainly, it seems to me, because after Teachers' College graduation, I chose not to pursue teaching. My interviewers inferred I was out of touch with current teaching methods and therefore not a suitable candidate. My confidence is at a low ebb and I am sure this position is my last chance.

Before applying for this job, I had no idea one-room schools still existed, especially in southern Ontario. Teachers' College, a one-year course with only minimal classroom teaching, has given me no practical preparation for such a job. I don't care. I need to teach two years out of five in order to obtain my permanent teaching certificate and, as I have spent over two years travelling with my husband as his job moved, I know time is of the essence. The most practical plan is to live in our hometown, Cobourg, and stay with my kind mother-in-law, Rosemonde Manning, who has offered to look after my now one-year-old son, Bruce. This job interview is my last chance at teaching in the area.

The young woman beside me definitely looks as though she is right out of Teachers' College. She goes in ahead of me and my anxiety increases exponentially as the minutes tick by. She is back out sooner than I expect and looks neither pleased nor discouraged.

When I hear my name called, I stand, determined to be calm. The not-too-spacious boardroom is panelled in dark wood, a long table down its centre. Seated around, looking weathered, some still in their barn clothes, are the Hamilton Township school board members.

"Mrs. Manning?" a man at the end of the table asks, a bit gruffly it seems to me.

"Sit down, sit down," someone else adds.

I sit in the end chair, acutely aware of six, or is it seven, sets of middle-aged male eyes scrutinizing me?

"I see you graduated from Toronto Teachers' College in 1961," the man at the end begins.

"Yes," I manage before my throat constricts. I know what the next question will be.

"And you didn't teach for the next two years as you went with your husband, James, to Northern Quebec," another man adds.

I nod, feeling my face reddening. The town schools did not take kindly to this information; rather, they seemed to hold it against me as some deficiency in my moral character.

"That would be Russell Manning's son?" another pipes up.

I nod again.

"And what would this husband of yours be doing in the wilds of northern Quebec?" another board member asks.

I can't help but wonder what this has to do with my teaching ability but dutifully reply. "He was installing computers in military bases on the Pinetree defence line," I say.

They seem impressed by this nodding and making notes. I am beginning to feel a little like Alice and I know I have not fallen down a rabbit hole.

"Do you have any experience in a one-room school?"

"Not directly," I reply, "but I did attend Baltimore Public School from grades Six to Eight and was in the senior room of the two-room school there."

"Miss Hogg," another man barked out, slapping his knee. "Now there was a crackerjack of a teacher."

"She taught in this very school," another adds.

"She did that—1957, I think it was," someone else offers.

More note scribbling. At this point, I want the interview to end. I can't see what this has to do with my suitability as a teacher for this school.

There is a momentary lull and I consider, for a second or two, jumping up and bolting. Am I so unsuitable that they are asking random general questions, nothing about how I would handle a given discipline situation or what approach I would take to a particular subject?

"Mrs. Manning?" The man closest to me is staring, tapping his index finger on the table. "Didn't you tap dance at the Baltimore Community Centre?"

I nod, feeling my throat tighten again. This is beyond ridiculous. "A long time ago," I manage to say. "The Judy Welch School of Dance."

"You were real good," someone else offers.

More scribbling.

I wait, feeling sweat running down my back, inside my Playtex girdle and, I'm sure, staining under my arms.

The man at the end of the table stands up. "That will be all," he says. "Thank you, Mrs. Manning."

By the time I am in the car and on the highway, tears blur my vision. I blink furiously and pound the steering wheel. I don't want to teach anyway. I'll find something else. Another job. Who needs teaching?

A week later, a letter from the Hamilton Township Board arrives at my mother-in-law's. I have the job. I will be principal and teacher of eight grades, the first school year to begin Tuesday September 3,

1963, and end Friday June 26, 1964. Remuneration $3000 a year with an extra $300 because of added principal's responsibilities.

After my initial euphoria subsides—I'm going to be a teacher with my own class, all eight grades of them—I refuse to be intimidated. I will figure it out. How to teach eight grades at the same time. How to prepare and organize lessons for umpteen courses starting with a lesson plan or plans. It has to be doable even in the eight summer weeks remaining.

Shortly after the interview, my designated board member, Mr. Moore, phones and says he can take me out to look at the school. My son and I are staying in Cobourg, my husband already away working at another Quebec site. My mother-in-law has generously offered me the use of her car, a red Honda mini. Mr. Moore says he will show me around the school and give me the key. A rush of excitement hits me. My school with my own key. Such a lofty responsibility and, as I soon find out, such a heavy work load.

We pick a day and time and, on another hot summer day, I drive along Highway 2, west of Cobourg, past the road north to the drive-in, past the Golden Miller restaurant as he has instructed, and find the school on the left, fields on either side. A one-storey brick building with a bell tower and a shed behind, the school has obviously seen better days. It appears that some years ago, the brick was painted and now, in many places, paint has worn off revealing faded bricks, many of them weather-pocked.

Mr. Moore grins broadly as I step out of my car. "Welcome," he says, "to the Front Road School West." The pride in his voice helps diminish the unease I am beginning to feel. Eight grades in one room. How will I ever manage? I follow behind through the front door past two closed doors and a storage area into the school room proper. The few schools I was in during my teaching training year were Toronto schools, most of them two storeys with a room for each grade, a staff room, an office and a generous foyer. Schools I attended as a child were much the same—both the four-room school in Charleswood, Manitoba, where I spent my first four years of schooling, and even the two-room Baltimore Public School where I was in the Senior room. Everything here, however, is in one room.

The six large, multi-paned windows are shut and a blast of heat hits us as we enter. As we pass through the narrow hallway into the main room, I can smell, but not identify, something decidedly unpleasant.

"Chemical toilets," Mr. Moore says, nodding back at them, "and don't you worry, the janitor makes sure they're kept clean during the year." He smiles. "Mrs. Carr, one of your students' mothers, is our first-rate janitor." He stops beside a substantial woodstove a couple of feet inside the door. I eye the long black pipe rising at least twice my height to become horizontal, ending where a patterned tin rim protects the plastered wall as it enters the chimney. "Yes," Mr. Moore continues, giving the stove's black surface a pat, "our Mrs. Carr cleans the school twice every week, and one of her older sons comes in to get the stove going in the winter."

He goes on to say that wood is stored in the shed behind the school and that there is always a good supply. The stove sits on a tin base separating it from the worn plank floor boards, a box for wood on one side. Everything is in pristine condition, not a stray ash in sight. I imagine it's different in winter, stray bits of bark strewn on the floor, ash coating the base beneath, possibly strewn farther out, onto the wood floor. I wonder who stokes it during the day.

"If you're wondering who tends your fire during cold days," Mr. Moore says, reading my mind, "it's one of the senior boys. No need to ask for a volunteer, they all know it has to be kept stoked." He rubs sweat from his forehead and runs his hand over his pants. "Hard to imagine on a day like today!"

I smile bravely and nod. Chemical toilets and a wood stove. What else?

The sink. I hadn't noticed it, being so absorbed by the long expanse of pipe from the stove. Rectangular porcelain in shape, the sink sits in a cabinet on the back wall beside a linoleum-topped table with decidedly weathered legs. An ancient-looking tap arches over its pocked interior, a long, reddish-brown stain beginning from where water hits the porcelain, ending at the partially rusted drain cover.

"Cold water tap," Mr. Moore says brightly and, as if it's an added bonus, "plus a pencil sharpener."

An ancient bookcase stands against the east wall, its books looking as though no one has touched them in decades. Large slate blackboards rise up between each of the three tall windows on both sides of the room, with the back wall entirely covered by their dark surface. They have been washed and gleam black in the light coming through the windows. I am at least pleased with the windows. Without them, it would indeed be dark and dreary. Little do I know that there are no storm windows and, in the winter when the wind blows from east or west, delicate piles of snow will collect on their sills.

The desks range from small in front to large at the back, the small ones being the kind you slide into from the right with a wooden writing surface extending around to the front, and a drawer under the seat. Halfway back, these change to desks with chairs and a table-like top for writing with a shelf underneath. I assume the different sizes carry with them status by age: possibly grades 1 to 4 in the more contained desks and grades 5 to 8 in the larger ones. I wonder what happens if there are too many juniors and not enough seniors, in which case small children will be sitting on chairs too big for them or, if the reverse, larger seniors will be obliged to squeeze into desks too small. I keep all this to myself as Mr. Moore shows me about the room.

The teacher's desk faces the student desks, blackboards filling the entire wall behind. The desk is made of solid wood with a centre drawer and two side compartments with doors. I sit down gingerly in the worn wooden chair behind it. It has arms and is on wheels. Again, I feel a rush of…power? Responsibility? Whatever it is, it quickly diminishes again to apprehension.

Mr. Moore throws a key onto the desk. "I'll just let you stay here and find your bearings," he says. "Need to get back to my chores." He gives me a little salute and strides out, slamming the door behind him.

I sit, staring at everything in the room, all of it run down, unkempt or just plain old. It's obvious the Board doesn't have much money, if any, for building upkeep. "Never mind," I say aloud. "You have a job, a whole school of your own. So get at it." I pull open the centre drawer and discover a large black hardcover attendance register.

Inside the front cover, a list written by the previous teacher. There will be children of varying numbers in each grade, a total of thirty-two students. I try not to panic. How can I possibly manage reading, spelling, literature, arithmetic, history, science and art for all these grades?

I will the queasiness in my stomach to leave and think back, briefly to my teachers' college year, the worst year of my life. I found it humiliating. Miss Belfry, who taught us primary-school skills and was obviously a former primary teacher herself, gave us each a printing book in which we were required to print the alphabet, upper and lower case. Matronly in shape with a coiffure of stiff blue hair, she was fastidious in her appraisal of our printing, circling in red any part of a letter that didn't align precisely. I was always in a hurry and thought the whole exercise ridiculous. As a result, I almost failed printing. As I try to come to terms with the enormity of the task in front of me, Miss Belfry's blue hair and my wretched printing book momentarily strike me as incredibly funny. Its significance was paramount at the time, given I could fail the subject if I didn't toe the line, while now it seems a mere speck compared to preparing for all subjects for eight grades.

It doesn't matter. I'm committed and I will succeed. It will be a one-year adventure, maybe two if things go well. Principal and teacher. Eight grades. Yes!

Victoria Hall by Norma Keith

WINNER OF THE FESTIVAL POETRY CONTEST

Maggie Harper

MY WEEK OF HAIKU

Sunday
A quarrel of quips
Quirky, quiet quills and questions
Laughter steals my breath....

Monday
Light brings a silence
to a tableau set for life
I experience

Tuesday
A burden so light
barely felt upon shoulders
yet weighted I was.

Wednesday
I heard your nibble
faint yet bold just feet away
Moving in are we?

Thursday
Buzzing by my ear
gentle inquisitive squeak
baby humming bird

Friday
One sigh becomes echoes
cascading into caverns
of unstoppered ears

Saturday
Iris solitaire
stunning white with purple beard
Creative splendour.

Marie Prins

SETTLERS' EFFECTS

Now that my husband and I have officially become senior citizens, it's time to downsize almost fifty years of possessions. So periodically we dive into the black holes of our house and drag out the contents of dark closets and kitchen shelves, dresser and desk drawers, bins packed away in the basement or garage. Once the contents are exposed, we quickly examine, sort, and discard piles of stuff that should have been recycled long ago. But inevitably we find things that bring our let's-get-it-done frenzy to a full stop—a Polaroid photo, an ancient birthday card, a hand-knit sweater three sizes too small. And then there's that one item that, like a lost puzzle piece, slides the panorama of a lifetime into a clearer and unequivocal focus.

Recently, in the bottom drawer of a rusty filing cabinet, I found a battered accordion file bound by a frayed elastic band. From its compartments, I pulled out an old manila envelope. Inside was a legal-sized, Canadian immigration document—the 1971 blue duplicate of our "Settlers' Effects." It had been filled out forty-five years ago by a customs agent in the hours after we crossed the border from the United States into Canada. In fading ink, its two type-written pages listed our household possessions and vehicles that accompanied us to this northern border.

Settlers? I asked myself as I unfolded the document and read its title. Weren't "settlers" people who migrated to rural areas after the pioneers arrived or "settled" the land by establishing farms and small towns? That wasn't us. When we arrived we did not erect a crude shanty or a log house somewhere in the backwoods. No, we moved into the basement apartment of a brick row house in the middle of busy Toronto, where streetcars rumbled past our door on Bathurst Street just south of Bloor.

We were "Landed Immigrants," as labelled on the small, oblong, identification cards we received in the mail two months after our applications were finalized. We lived in a neighbourhood of immigrants, many who shopped like us in Kensington Market to the south and Honest Ed's north of our building. But even if we were not "settlers" by the dictionary definition, that copy of our "Settlers' Effects" revealed the beginning of a settlement story, the first chapter of our life in a new country.

In 1971, we had moved to Canada scarcely three months after I graduated from college south of Chicago, where we had lived on campus in a student apartment. During the first two years of married life, we had purchased the settlers' effects ticked off on that immigration document. The "living room suite" was an ugly grey sofa and a solid mahogany desk, plus a captain's chair rescued from the furnace room. Our "bedroom suite" was a mattress with a box spring and an antique dresser with a wavy mirror, our "kitchen set" a small oak table with four matching chairs. Everything had been bought for under $40 at garage sales. Ed had spent hours scraping off paint and refinishing the wooden pieces. As for the electronics, we imported an RCA television with tubes, a Lafayette "hi-fi" set, and my Underwood typewriter. Of course, we also had bedding, clothing, linens, kitchen utensils, "chinaware" (my everyday Corning ware), glassware, and pots and pans. The "pictures" must have been Ed's early art pieces. And we had boxes of books, a rug, a lamp, a vacuum cleaner, a sewing machine, and a fan. Plus fishing and camping equipment, which I think was Ed's pole and tackle box.

That was it! We packed everything next to Ed's 1967 Honda motorbike in a small U-Haul truck we shared with friends also moving north. It followed our 1964 Ford Fairlane across the Blue

Water Bridge to a booth at the Sarnia border crossing. There we declared to an inscrutable officer that we wished to immigrate into Canada. He instructed us to pull over, and a polite customs agent ushered us into a stuffy room. In silence, perched nervously on folding chairs; we surrendered our immigration applications, along with notarized copies of birth and marriage certificates, health records, education records, and, most importantly, Ed's offer of employment. Then we carefully counted out the $1000 cash needed to demonstrate we could support ourselves until our first paycheques arrived. Without comment, the agent added up our "points" and determined they met the requirement necessary to immigrate.

Two hours later, we were back on the road with our settlers' effects, headed to Toronto. Eight months later, we abandoned that shanty apartment and purchased a small house in Scarborough for $18,500. After four-and-a-half years living by the Bluffs, we moved back to the downtown core and began to renovate a derelict boarding house in Cabbagetown. A dozen years later we pulled up stakes to raise our two young children in a rural setting reminiscent of our New Jersey childhood environments, where I had freely roamed the woods by my house and Ed had caught snakes in the fields behind his. A back-to-the-land urge led us along the 401 to the edge of a town 140 kilometres east of Toronto, where fate or foolishness induced us to buy another run-down house on 1.5 acres not far from Lake Ontario. Maybe that's when we became settlers.

Next to that old filing cabinet in our upstairs library, the bookshelves hold Rodale's *High-Yield Gardening,* Dick Raymond's *Joy of Gardening,* and books on natural pest and disease control. Our property is technically within town limits, for we benefit from town water and sewage. But it is surrounded on two sides by woods and a stream. That first spring, as soon as the frost left the large, overgrown vegetable garden behind our house, Ed fired up our brand-new BCS rototiller and "ploughed the field."

A decade after we moved to Colborne, an elderly gentleman pulled into our driveway one morning. He thrust into my hands an old photograph glued onto a battered cardboard frame. It was an eight-by-ten-inch sepia portrait of nine members of the Scott Family, all dressed in black. For it, they had patiently posed in front of our house while an unseen photographer snapped the shot with his wooden bellows camera perched on a tripod. The year may have been 1899, the occasion perhaps the funeral of Reuben Bartlett Scott, the family patriarch, who had passed away that March.

Our house is the historical Scott House, one of the few remaining octagonal houses built in the mid-1800s by followers of Ogden Fowler, who believed that a round house did not trap "bad air" and infect its inhabitants. R. B. Scott, rumoured to have possessed a copy of his book *The Octagon: A Home for All*, constructed this unique building as a wedding present for his wife Maria Hyuck in 1853. Forty-five-plus years after we lugged our settlers' effects across the border, many of them now furnish a house built by R.B., who was the son of another American immigrant, Reuben Scott. Our captain's chair sits grandly in the old kitchen, the mahogany desk in the tiny office, the walnut-veneered bureau with its wavy mirror in a bedroom. Every day we still eat off the Corning "chinaware" now officially deemed vintage on e-Bay.

R. B.'s father, Reuben, and his large family had lived in Vermont before moving to Madrid, New York, in the early 1800s. After the death of his father, Reuben immigrated in 1810 to Upper Canada (Ontario) with his mother, Anne Hawley Scott, and his three youngest brothers. They likely gave most of their household belongings to family left behind and packed only what they could carry—clothing, bedding, and small, personal items too precious to part with, plus cooking utensils and food for the journey. These meagre possessions were probably loaded onto a crowded bateau at Ogdensburg NY and rowed along the St. Lawrence River to

Kingston by French-Canadian *voyageurs*. When the Scott family reached Kingston, their luggage may have been inspected at the customs house, and most likely their settlers' effects were not taxed, just checked over to make sure nothing unlawful was being smuggled into Canada.

The octagon remained in the Scott family until 1967 when it was sold to that gentleman who gave us the photograph. He in turn sold it to the man whose "renovations" took us twenty-five years to undo, one room at a time. So while we may not have lived in a log cabin with a dirt floor like the settlers, we did "camp" in our house for a long time while Ed rewired and re-plumbed, scraped stucco off walls and painted them, stripped trim around windows and doors, re-did floors, and patched and painted the whole exterior of the house.

After I discovered the document that listed our settlers' effects, I became interested in the arrival stories of other immigrants to Canada. What possessions did they bring with them? What was left behind? Two of Canada's earliest writers, sisters Catherine Parr Traill and Susanna Moodie (née Strickland), wrote of their passages to Canada in 1832. As wives of British army officers, they sailed as cabin passengers across the ocean. They packed their possessions into trunks and crates: clothing, bedding, books, and "kitchenware," plus food for the journey. Presumably not much different than that of the people cramped below in steerage, except in quantity and quality.

They "crossed the border" when their ships entered the mouth of the St. Lawrence River and sailed to Quebec City. As cabin passengers they were not considered health risks and did not have to disembark at Grosse Isle, although their bedding had to be washed there by maidservants, to insure it was not infected with the dreaded cholera disease. A few days later in Montreal, their luggage was inspected by customs.

In 1855, Catherine Parr Traill published *The Canadian Settler's Guide.* In it she advised immigrants to pack "good clothing and plenty of good shoes and boots…as for personal luggage you will have no freight to pay… Do not bring furniture or 'iron-ware' since the freightage, warehouse room, custom-house duties…will have made them dear bargains." She further suggested that if "a list of the contents of each box or trunk be put within the lid, and showed to the custom-house officer, (it) will save a great deal of unpacking and trouble." This advice came out of hard personal experience as the Traills' luggage had been held up at the customs house in 1832. During that time Catherine contracted cholera. Mercifully she recovered from her brush with death. Perhaps she would not have gotten so sick if their own luggage had been properly packed, labelled, and hustled quickly out of customs.

Whether or not the Moodies ran into the same difficulties or paid duty on their settlers' effects is not recorded in Susanna's writings. However, when living north of Cobourg that first year, Susanna complained bitterly in her book *Roughing It in the Bush* about belligerent neighbours borrowing and never returning their few, hard-to-replace possessions that they had brought with them from England.

Like the Scotts, the Traills, and the Moodies, most immigrants over the past three hundred years have arrived in Canada with some settlers' effects. The early settlers brought only a few crates and trunks, especially if they sailed by boat either across the ocean or fled as Loyalists along the Lake Champlain waterway. Others, particularly slaves escaping via the Underground Railroad in the mid-1800s, were lucky to cross the border with their lives and maybe a small bundle. In the late 1800s, as transportation across the Atlantic and Pacific oceans improved and as the railroad extended westward, many settlers of all nationalities packed boxes and crates, some shipped later by freight. After World War II, war brides from England and

Europe's liberated countries brought with them their small children, who had not seen their Canadian fathers. Dutch farming families packed huge wooden *kists* that were loaded into the holds of troop ships bound for Canada. Customs officials joked that they brought everything but the kitchen sink. But most immigrants until that time came with very little money and few belongings.

As for paperwork, in the 1800s immigration forms were just names listed on a ship's manifest. By the early 1900s, immigration documents were one or two pages long (Form 30A). Settlers' effects were verbally declared, and visually inspected by customs agents. For the most part, they were duty-free.

Since the end of World War I, over a half dozen federal government departments have overseen immigration and its growth of documentation. A number of acts and regulations have redefined who can immigrate to Canada and what qualifies as "Personal Effects" (renamed by Canada Border Services Agency). In a nutshell, today's immigrants can import duty-free household and personal items if actually owned, possessed, and used abroad by them prior to arrival in Canada. For advice on how to pack and label all one's goods, there are websites and blogs reminiscent of Traill's directive from 1855. Most advise that filling out the forms correctly is all border agents really wish to see.

Quite a few immigrants today still arrive like those in the 1800s. Refugees from the Middle East or Africa, asylum seekers at airports, and "border runners" at unsupervised land-crossings carry with them just a backpack or a suitcase. Inside their luggage are clothes and a few precious personal items. Recently I was privileged to be told the stories of two families who had immigrated to Canada in 2015.

In the first story, two Iranian sisters recounted that when they left a refugee camp in Turkey, they managed to bring with them all their books, as well as many letters and photographs. "My luggage was filled with Iran's soul," said one. As she told her story, the sister laughed and insisted that one suitcase was completely filled with her sister's dresses. They had also packed small going-away presents, such as an ornate glass jar containing a tiny letter, and a necklace with an *amen* bird on its pendant. The lore of the bird is that if one makes a wish and then sees this sparrow-like bird in the sky, that wish will come true. Since these women had jobs in the refugee camp, they were able to convert their last salaries from Turkish lira into Canadian dollars and were thus able to bring a little bit of cash with them.

In the other story, a Syrian mother and her three children who came to Canada in late December 2015 told a sadder tale. Five years before being privately sponsored as refugees, they had left everything they owned in Homs, Syria, when they fled with the clothes on their backs. They had nothing when they arrived in Lebanon and very little when they travelled to Canada from the refugee camp. There were no personal items like books, toys, dolls, or games. All they brought with them were winter clothes they had purchased with money sent by their sponsors. Even their cell phone, which had been a lifeline to family members, had to be discarded because of its poor condition. When asked what she wished she had been able to save, the mother answered like anyone who loses their lifetime belongings in fire or flood—her papers: pictures, birth certificates, memorabilia that can never be replaced. Then she added that she wished she was able to have her husband arrive with her. But he had been missing for five years before they came to Canada.

This mother's haunting story has too often been the immigrant's story, from the Irish Potato Famine immigrant stories of those who in 1847 arrived by boat and often died at Grosse Isle, to the "displaced persons" stories of those who arrived totally alone at Pier 21 after World War II, to the Vietnamese boat people's stories of those who, after escaping civil war and pirates in the South Asia Sea, arrived at our airports in 1975. Since the early 1600s, there have been innumerable untold stories of immigrants who came here from all over the world to escape poverty, famine, war, slavery, and persecution. No matter how much or how little they brought with them, all left someone behind.

Whatever settlers' effects immigrants bring to Canada, they help the newcomer bridge the familiar life of their birth country to the unknown one before them. A piece of clothing or jewellery, a keepsake from a dead loved one, a photograph, a family heirloom—all these precious items carry a story and contain a history, thus helping to keep one's identity intact. Physically, psychologically, and often economically, life in a new country is often very challenging. "Home! The word had ceased to belong to my present—it was doomed to live forever in the past," wrote Susanna Moodie. "For what emigrant ever regarded the country of his exile as his home? The heart acknowledges no other home than the land of its birth." The Strickland sisters suffered overwhelming nostalgia and homesickness while they adjusted to this foreign land. I can only imagine how immigrants from other countries long for their birthplace, despite the poverty and horrors they may have escaped, and despite the tremendous difficulty of their journey here.

Even though our own crossing was undramatic given the similarities of life in Canada and the United States, my husband and I often considered returning "home" to live closer to family we dearly missed. For one reason or another, we never took that step. And then after many years, when our "belongings" had greatly increased, we realized that this noun had become a verb. We now *belonged*...to this land, to this vast country called Canada. It had finally, gradually, become "home." For our children had been born here, and as they grew up, our hearts had taken root in this northern soil that had moulded our lives and beings into a Canadian shape, the shape of immigrants in a new land, settlers who became citizens.

Kim Aubrey

WINTER GRACE

Thank you for the places I have landed
that have taught this Bermuda girl to love
winter—Saskatoon's bright constant snow,
how the South Saskatchewan River broke
and healed itself over and over. Waking
to hoar frost's crystalline magic. Sun dogs.
Ice that forms in air, improbable stars.

And now the northern shores of Lake Ontario
where I can tread a tawny frozen landscape,
sand and pebbles ice adhered into textured
slabs. Where waves bless drab dry shrubs
with a glistening coat, and black-and-white
mergansers bob and plunge in water
that today sings island turquoise.

Places where I have learned to love
the hard stuck parts of myself, to allow water
to melt me, mend me, lend me its shine.

Winter from a painting by Lori Felix

Wally Keeler

TREE AT HULL'S CORNER

Large, thick
with the nourishment of a generous soil
your branches
full armed green
tripping wild breezes
weaving sun and seed
to clothe the fields.

When summer fled like a skittish kitten
your summer suit of green grace
went hippie crispy
lying about in meadows,
unemployed.

While friends attended Sunday School
learning to ask unanswerable questions
proofs of things greater than themselves
I played in the shelter of your shade.
You were my favourite tree.
We cast our fantasies in the grass;
you occupied the brain-forts I had built
with invaders from your boughs.

You were strong-stemmed.
Affluence failed to soften you;
winter spears were harmless

to your bare courage.

I am older now,
remembering the outreach of your branches
holding my thoughts for the inspection
of wind in the wild.

Yesterday, I went to you
and found an off-ramp
entombing your roots
and tires rollin' rollin' rollin'
over our favourite forts
on a free
way.

Christopher Black

THE MAN AT THE CHURCH

I have the habit of going for a walk in the morning, walking silently, in safe solitude, simply breathing, legs stretching out, arms keeping time, feeling a different rhythm of life. It helps me deal with the increasing agitation I experience on hearing the daily news of wars, corruption, of people alienated from each other, from themselves, of a dying world.

My routine takes me up the paved road to the top of the hill, the hill that dominates the small Ontario town in which I live, which lies spread out along the river that winds its way south to the great lake. There, looking down over the valley below, sits a church, a cathedral almost, St. Mary's, the Catholic church that dominates all the other churches in the town by its majesty, as if to show the Protestants what a real church should look like. Sometimes, when the mood strikes me, I stop to look at it, to admire it, for though I am not a religious man, the ceremonies, the architecture, the art and iconography of the church are to me mysterious and beautiful. The rest of it creates no interest for me. I find my salvation in the nature that surrounds me, not in the mythology of its creation.

Or so I thought, until something happened that caused me to reconsider the mysteries of the world.

One day, in early June I think it was, the year of the great spring rains, I decided to get up earlier than usual to take my walk. I couldn't sleep. The sun was rising. It promised to be a dramatic overture to the day; a blue sky covering green hills awash in bird songs sung in many different keys, accompanied by the soft rustling harmony of countless leaves whispering in the warming breeze.

The locals of the town were beginning to stir. The occasional vehicle, a pickup truck, a run-down car, passed me by on the way to market or work, but no one else was walking along the street that led from my house to the main street, then up the hill heading toward the edge of town and the tower of St. Mary's that held the big bell, the bell that rang out several times a day calling the faithful to prayer.

When I got to the top of the hill and stood in the shadow of the entrance to the church with its big wooden double doors, flanked on each side by a Norman tower graced with several stained glass windows, the left tower with the spire and cross at its top, the right containing the bell, I paused in my walk, put my hands in my pockets, looked up to the bell tower and wondered just how big that bell was. It was while pondering this question that I heard the clunky thud of the church doors opening and closing, and on looking over I saw a figure coming toward me dressed in the black habit and beard of a Jesuit, which struck me as odd as there were no Jesuits in the parish that I had heard of.

I could not see his face. It was hidden in the shadows of the old-fashioned cowl he had covering his head. He approached me slowly with a steady step until he stood in front of me. For some reason—the angle of the sun, the weight of his cowl—I could not see his face apart from the black beard, tight, grim lips, the tip of a hooked nose above the moustache. The rest vanished into the darkness of the hood he wore despite the warming of the day.

I greeted him with the usual "Hello, nice day, isn't it?" or some such thing that we say without thinking when meeting strangers. It gets muddled in my head now, but there was no response. The figure stood in front of me without moving, very still, like one of those human mannequins tourists are delighted by in Europe, a Marie Antoinette, a silver clown, or a marble Dante with his book. He seemed very solid at first, but then I noticed that his form shimmered in the light as do those mirages of dark water that lie across the road in the summer heat and vanish as soon as you see them.

The silence of this apparition, for so it seemed to be, unnerved me. I stepped back, took my hands from my pockets and prepared to retreat. But the form continued to stand there without a sound or movement. Now more unnerved, I challenged him with, "Are you all right, Father? Can I help you?"

There was no sound, no movement, except for the subtle, almost undetectable, shimmer I referred to before, but then a voice that seemed to come from some distant place, some distant time, cried out, as if wailing at a death, "What have you done? What have you done?" And with that, the figure raised his right hand and pointed it, while turning his body, calling out all the while, "What have you done?"

He spoke in French, a language I understand, but with an accent I had not heard before. I still am not sure if I understood him correctly, but I was so transfixed by the voice and the movement as I followed his hand pointing at the world around us that I seemed to comprehend him nevertheless and was surprised when a feeling of intense melancholy swept over me. Tears filled my eyes, and I fell to the ground at his feet, overwhelmed by sudden grief.

He stopped turning, looked at me, lowered his hand, and bowed his head. He began to turn away from me. I reached out to try to stop him, but my hand passed through air. I struggled to my feet, wiping away the tears that still bathed my eyes, trying to restore my equilibrium, but he did not stop and kept walking back toward the doors, his shoulders and back bent, his head lowered, and through my own tears, I saw signs of a man sobbing uncontrollably. I managed to shout out, "Who are you?"—perhaps an unfair thing to ask when I was not even sure who I was. "Your name?" And protested, "I've done nothing, just lived."

He stopped, turned his head to look at me over his shoulder, and with a voice that came from a deep abyss said, again, "What have you done? What have you done? Terrible things, terrible things," each word a moan, or so it seemed, as he turned his head away and walked slowly back to the door of the church, where his shimmering figure merged with the door and dissolved into the shadows as if he had never been.

The encounter so disturbed me that I felt paralyzed for some seconds until I regained my senses and, shaken, decided to turn back toward home. As I walked slowly back into the town, I reflected on the melancholy encounter, what it meant, that question from the past demanding an explanation from the present about our destruction of the future. For that was what it was. Of that I am sure.

Upon relating what happened to my wife, my friends, my doctor, explanations were quick in coming. My wife looked at me oddly. Some said outright I was a liar and pulling their leg. Some religious people took it as a proof of God, a warning from the Almighty, some as the visitation of an angel. The Catholics quickly claimed it as a miracle, proof of the true martyrdom of Jean de Brébeuf in 1649, whose ghost this undoubtedly was. I hear the matter has been raised at the Vatican, and the students of the local schools now discuss the work of the Jesuits in the area three hundred years ago. The Protestants, in protest, proclaimed it to be God's clear condemnation of the Roman church. The new-agers stated categorically that it was the manifestation of some spirit of nature, mourning its steady destruction, and, of course the psychiatrists, my psychiatrists, determined, on clinical evidence, that it was a hallucination, a psychotic episode; that I had experienced a break with reality. I cannot comment on these theories. When I try, my attempts are considered just more evidence that my mind is unbalanced. And who am I to say it is not.

Several months have since passed. I have learned now to keep quiet, to agree with them that I was ill but now am well. I was finally allowed home after a long period of analysis, allowed to return to the birds, the sky, the whispering leaves, to again walk past the church on a warm spring or summer's day, as if nothing had ever happened. But, each time I do, each time I see those doors, when the light is right, the sky is blue, the leaves whispering, and no one else is there, I still see the man at the church, and hear that ancient voice moaning and asking over and over again, "What have you done? What have you done? Terrible things, terrible things."

Derek Paul

MY FIRST CONVERSATION WITH A BEAVER

During my early September absence from the cottage on Lake Temiskaming, just north of Haileybury, the local beaver family had cut every poplar tree in sight on the property's several acres. I surveyed the damage. It was too late to save the poplars, but still I wondered, "If only I could confront the beavers!"

At dusk I had a sudden premonition that they might be coming again in search of just one more tree. There wasn't another to cut down, but beavers are optimists. So I silently slipped down to the northernmost of the beaches on the property, which I felt was their likely landing place. This beach is quite small, and is bounded by high rocks north, south and west. To my great delight, as I was still climbing down the rocks, I saw the whole beaver family swimming around the point of land north of the beach. By the time I had reached the water's edge, the leader was already positioned straight out from the shore. He flapped a special signal telling the others to go home. They all turned tail at once, leaving him alone to face this giant on the shore.

By then I had picked up a stout stick and was standing, my feet apart, right arm outstretched to the top of my staff, its lower end close to my right foot. It was an attempt at resembling Neptune, whose mythic picture I had once seen in a children's illustrated book, commanding the waters, an image hard to recreate in haste.

The beaver—clearly the patriarch—then began his survey. He swam slowly in a large circle of about twenty yards' radius, at the near point coming within ten yards of my position and at the far point fifty yards. Not once but twice he circled, taking many minutes to complete this whole movement. I never moved a muscle. Then he stopped at the far point and turned to face me. "Krrriickk," he uttered. Then again, "Krrriickk." Beaver language is a little beyond my ken. "Krrxrxriickk," I answered ungrammatically. "Krrriickk," he replied. "Krxrxrriickck," I responded incompetently. This time he didn't answer, so I repeated my *krxrxrriick* so as to improve upon the previous one.

It must have been good enough to make him curious. He started to swim again, but now in a straight line toward me, and even slower than before. Still I never moved a muscle. He just went on coming, until at last his belly struck the pebbles six feet away from me, whereupon he gazed for some minutes on this monster that never moved. But he seemed to be defending his territory. Then slowly he retreated backwards, never taking his eyes off me. At twenty yards he turned for home, but I stayed on, motionless, marvelling at Creation.

Donna Wootton

WANDERING BEAVER

I wonder where the beaver's gone
Who walked on lonely beaches
In January through the thaw?

Now when the wind howls
And heavy snow abounds
The landscape is solid white.

Seems a ludicrous sighting
That large slick black rodent
Gnawing on sticks on sandy shores.

Its image fixed on nickel coins
Removed from dam and wetlands
Still a familiar profile.

Alan Bland

OLD JUBAL AND HOMER

Northumberland County is mostly peaceful these days, notwithstanding that there is a federal penitentiary in Warkworth, but it wasn't always that way. Back around 1950 there were some shenanigans up in what is now Trent Hills where some of the old farm families, descended from the original settlers, still lived according to their own rules.

***

If you had asked anyone around town none of them would have remembered exactly how it had started. Some said it was when Old Jubal's hogs got out and rooted up all the vegetables in Homer's wife's garden. But others would say that the hogs wouldn't have got out if that old rotted-out oak tree of Homer's hadn't come down in the storm and busted the fence between his wife's veggie patch and Old Jubal's hog run.

It didn't help things along when Homer decided that the only way to placate his wife and stop the hogs gorging on her prize veggies was to shoot those darned hogs. And that's what he did. All three of them. Bang! Bang! Bang!

Now Old Jubal had been in town picking up supplies, some of which he would no longer need as his hogs had permanently lost their appetites.

When Old Jubal arrived back from town, his rusty pickup clanking and wheezing up the rutted lane and splashing through the puddles left by the storm, he could sense something was wrong. He'd stayed in town until the storm had passed, one of those sharp and nasty ones that came with a downpour of rain and winds that whipped the trees in every direction until some of them just gave up and fell down. Like the one between Old Jubal's and Homer's farms.

Homer's boys, Wilbur and Walter, had hefted the hogs back onto Old Jubal's side of the property line but there was no hiding those bullet holes, right between the eyes on each of those three hogs. When Jubal went to visit Homer he let it be known that an explanation was expected as to how he had three murdered hogs in his yard and why Homer was sitting on his front porch with that big Winchester rifle over his knee and his two strapping sons, Wilbur and Walter, sitting one on each side of him.

Well, as you can imagine, that meeting didn't go too well, what with Old Jubal wanting payment for his three hogs and Homer telling him to just get them to the abattoir before they went off and would only be fit for the landfill. Old Jubal pointing out that the abattoir couldn't take them as they were already dead and Homer pointing out that he knew that Old Jubal had butchered a few hogs in his barn every year, so why not now?

A kind of compromise was worked out. Wilbur and Walter helped Old Jubal get those hogs into the barn where they were hung and dressed. Homer bought all the meat from one and filled his freezer while Old Jubal took care of the other two. And then some more money changed hands from Homer to Old Jubal.

Walter and Wilbur got out the chainsaws and cleaned up the oak that had fallen on the fence and started the whole shebang in the first place. And that should have been the end of it.

Except Old Jubal still felt he'd been wronged by Homer. While Old Jubal lived alone on his hardscrabble ten acres, that didn't mean he was always going to be alone, and so he phoned his cousins, Clancey and Yancey, who were well known as animal trappers.

Homer and his wife, and their boys Wilbur and Walter, had been to town to buy feed for the chickens that Homer's wife raised, while the two boys went to the matinee at the new Aron movie theatre in Campbellford.

As Homer drove his old rusted pickup down his lane and over the ruts that had dried out after the earlier storm, he bounced into the yard feeling something was amiss. Homer, his wife, and Wilbur and Walter climbed down from the pickup in time to see a pair of foxes, blood and feathers on their mouths, run for the hole in the fence—that was still to be fixed—out of the yard and into the fields.

Once Homer and his wife entered the chicken run they could see the extent of the havoc the foxes had wrought. Not a single chicken was left alive. The few that had escaped into the yard were all maimed and bloody.

Homer looked across the yard to his neighbour's property where Old Jubal and his cousins Clancey and Yancey sat on the porch with shotguns over their knees.

It wasn't over yet, but that's how it had started…

Summer Harvest by Norma Keith

Tom Pickering

A FAMILY LINK TO NORTHERN ONTARIO

Canada's growth in numbers and in economic development owes much to our southern neighbour. Starting in the 1770s and continuing into the early 1800s, more than 50,000 Americans loyal to the British Crown moved north across the border. A much larger and later wave of American immigration to Canada took place about a century later when Wilfrid Laurier's Liberal government decided to populate the prairies through promotion of free 160-acre parcels of land. Americans from western states crossed the border into the prairie provinces to occupy and develop this land. For Americans from western states who already knew the climate and terrain, the move north was definitely appealing. The University of Regina estimates that roughly 330, 000 American pioneers settled in Saskatchewan between 1905 and 1923. Some of those were born in the United States, while others were European immigrants who had first tried to settle south of the border.

Not as well documented and far less certain in actual numbers was the participation of Americans in the development of Northern Ontario's mining industry. The relocation of my maternal great-grandparents from Chicago to Cobalt is an example. Ironically, it was the building of a railway to serve existing settlements in the agricultural Clay Belt of Cochrane District in northeastern Ontario that launched a frenzy of mining exploration and extraction originating in Cobalt and then extending to locations further north such as Porcupine and Kirkland Lake.

In 1903 silver was discovered during construction of the Temiskaming & Northern Ontario Railway (T&NO) linking North

Bay to New Liskeard, on the shores of Lake Temiskaming. The accidental discovery was not so surprising when one considers ore deposits could extrude up to ground level. One story from that period has a blacksmith named Fred LaRose throwing a hammer at a nearby inquisitive fox, missing it, but knocking off a piece of rock to expose a vein of silver that would become the site of the LaRose mine.

By 1905 there were sixteen mines in the vicinity of Cobalt. By 1911, the year with the largest production of silver at 30 million ounces, the number of mines was estimated to be around one hundred. Influx of people to the area grew enormously, especially with the railway extended to Cobalt and New Liskeard by 1905 and to Cochrane by 1908. In his book, *Link with a Lonely Land: the Temiskaming and Northern Ontario Railway*, Michael Barnes refers to a "very respectable total of 359, 861 passengers carried on the line in 1906." After silver ore discoveries, Cobalt's population grew to over 10,000. The amount of business activity attached to mining was reflected in the listing of mining shares on the stock market in Toronto. The *Cobalt Daily Nugget* newspaper edition of April 3, 1911, informs readers that "Transactions in Cobalt and Porcupine shares for the week ending 31st March on the Toronto market totalled 1,861,000 shares, having a value of $1,196,113.77 as follows" and continues to list share prices for forty-nine mining companies.

News of the discovery and its scope was reported to the rest of Canada, the United States, and the world at large. My maternal great-grandfather Alfred A. Smith of Chicago certainly took notice. In the summer of 1908, he left his partnership in the Continental Casualty Company to be manager of the Badger Mine in Cobalt, Ontario. Family lore has it he won a stake in the mine in a poker game. It's possible his company may have bought shares in the mine and wanted one of their own on site. The reason he went was never recorded but the motivation to go was undeniable. His wife, Edith, and his three daughters, Genevieve, Dorothy, and Helen, accompanied him on the journey from Chicago to their new home. Quite a change in scenery and setting. In 1910, Chicago was the second largest city in the United States with a population of 2,185,000 people. By comparison, Toronto's population in 1911 was listed between 375,000 and 380,000 according to various sources.

Genevieve's recollections of the era include their first Christmas dinner and the assortment of guests. "The boys and men in our end of the camp who could not get home for the holidays were invited to come for dinner, so twenty-five of us sat down at the table. It was a Christmas to remember always. Our guests were from all parts of the world. There was a man from Cape Town, South Africa; an engineer from New York City; a chap from England who was educated in Hong Kong; Norman and Bill Fischer from New Zealand; Anson and Harry Carroll from Nebraska; Harry Stewart from Montreal; our teacher from England; and the rest were from Toronto or Chicago."

Editions of the *Daily Nugget* make reference to American participation in exploration and mining. Only selected editions from 1911 remain accessible; however, they retain a glimpse of the participation and level of interest from Americans, and Chicagoans in particular. A March 27 article titled "Chicagoans Attracted by Porcupine Claims" mentions purchase of a claim by Chicagoans and goes further to say, "To date there has not been much capital from the Windy City invested in the Northern Ontario camps. It has been turning the other way. Chicagoans have been making money in Northern Ontario." The article carries on to say the most conspicuous example of this is the participation of Mr. W. S. Edwards of Chicago who grubstaked (provided funds on promise of a share in the discovery) the prospectors who found gold at the site of what would become the Dome mine. The Nugget's June 24 edition detailed a planned excursion of eight hundred businessmen from Chicago to Cobalt organized by Mr. M.G. Grover, a well-known mining hand, as well as a second excursion for two hundred businessmen from Detroit and Cleveland. Whether those excursions took place and at the scale imagined is not known.

In the same year, a tour of Cobalt, New Liskeard, and Cochrane was organized to receive visiting members of the Toronto Board of Trade. Up to 150 members, including the President of the Board, were expected to arrive in the area for a tour of the mines, farmland, and the T&NO railway, and to be entertained at banquets in New Liskeard and Cochrane. Speakers and hosts were recruited from local boards of trade and representatives of the mining and farming community. Attendees included local dignitaries such as the MPP for Temiskaming and the chairman of the T&NO railway. The opportunity for investment was promoted and visiting board of trade members were suitably impressed. Whatever came out of that enthusiasm may not have materialized as imagined, but what is certain is that success in Cobalt launched further exploration and subsequent investment into mining operations throughout the region. Both the scope and longevity of those subsequent successes is noteworthy. For example, the Dome mine that was established in 1910 was reported to be entering its 107th year of operation according to a *Timmins Press* article dated July 20, 2016. Kirkland Lake, also not far from Cobalt, still has mines in operation.

In those early days, dynamite was an essential mining tool and many references are made to it. Genevieve tells the story of a miner entering a small dynamite house behind a bungalow belonging to their friends, the Hewitts. "The miner evidently had a lighted pipe and was followed by his faithful dog. In seconds, the Hewitts, sleeping peacefully, found their bed rolling across the room, the windows shattered and the whole house shaken from a rectangle to a quadrangle. Part of the dog was found but that was all." Despite this unfortunate explosion, she elaborates that it was a common thing around the camp to see a miner with dynamite sticks in the top of his boots to thaw out before being used. This ubiquitous presence of dynamite in the town and surrounding area is reflected in a brief comment from an article in the *Chicago Tribune* from August 13, 1905. "Prospectors now are searching surrounding regions for many miles and dynamite explosions are heard in all directions from morning to night."

The *Nugget*'s reporting often referred to equipment installed at particular mines, or to shafts being built. Genevieve and her sisters got a close-up look of their own from some of the larger mines. She says, "We were treated one day to a trip down the shaft, over five-hundred feet where the Crown Reserve found its biggest silver vein and Mr. Sam Cohen and his brother Julius explained the workings to us. As we were under a lake, the water dripped through the rock so oilskins were a necessary protection. Not to be outdone, the manager of the Shamrock Mine had a party and we were once again underground, but this time it was dry and very dusty. We learned after this trip that some miners quit as it was a bad omen for a woman to go into a mine. At the Badger, from the start, silver was plentiful so it was decided to build a plant. The day the plant was put into action we three girls each had a job to perform. I pulled the throttle of the compressor, Dorothy started the hoist and Helen sent the dynamo into action. It was a wonderful day for us and everything went smoothly."

A frequent danger in those days was fire. My grandmother's memoirs include mention of their home's rescue from forest fire followed by report of fire within the town one day later. "Next morning early, we heard dynamite blasts and the sky had a funny colour. So, on thinking it over, we decided that the town of Cobalt was on fire and sure enough, it was an inferno. When the dry goods store was blown up, bolts of material flew into the air with streamers giving it a weird picture. Some lives were lost and the town destroyed but it seemed in no time a completely new Cobalt took its place and business continued as usual."

Sometimes things don't work as planned and unfortunately for the Smiths and their employees, the Badger's production petered out. Opened in 1907, all mining operations became officially abandoned by the end of 1912 when the mine had produced only 3,475 ounces of silver. Sadly, the company could not locate another vein after a promising beginning. As Genevieve put it succinctly, "Fortunes were made and lost overnight."

For the Smith family, their northern Ontario adventure was over when Mr. Smith made the decision to move south to Toronto. The family's contribution to Canadian society didn't end there, nor did those of some of their American friends who also lived in Cobalt. Anson Carroll, a friend from Nebraska, served with the Royal Flying Corps in WWI and later worked in the aeronautical inspection division of de Havilland Aircraft Company in Downsview, Ontario. Mr. Smith went on to partner with boyhood friends from Wisconsin who wanted their Bay City, Michigan company to expand to Canada. The Sovereign Construction Company of Bay City, later renamed Aladdin Homes, made ready-cut or prefabricated homes advertised with the slogan "Built in a Day." Aladdin Homes became parent company to the Canadian Aladdin Company Limited located in the CPR building at King and Yonge Street. Genevieve completed business college in 1916 and proceeded to work as her father's secretary and then office manager. In a very fitting irony, the company had dealings with the mining industry in Northern Ontario they had come to know. Genevieve commented, "We were doing a thriving business at the International Nickel Company in Sudbury, supplying ready-cut homes for their employees."

Gerry Malloy

THE LOST ART OF GOING FOR A DRIVE

"Let's go get some ice cream," my dad would say. It didn't happen often. Usually it was on a hot summer night, when the air was still and the humidity oppressive and he knew sleep wouldn't come, even though it was well past my bedtime. We'd climb into his big, black sedan, roll down all the windows, and motor off sedately, meandering along the river road to the curb-service snack-bar that my aunt and uncle ran in the next town. And I would savour the coolness of the air swirling around the cabin, and the smell of the fresh-cut hay in the fields we passed, and the sheer joy of just going for a drive.

That was the point, you see. The ice-cream cone was just a rationalization—albeit a pleasant one. But we could have gotten ice cream two blocks from home. The real reward was the drive.

Those memories of carefree youth came flooding back last summer as I cruised slowly along a nearby lakeshore, top down on the convertible I was driving, my sweetheart comfortable in the seat beside me, and our dog happy in the back. The purple and orange remains of sunset still lingered in the western sky, and we could hear the peepers chirping all around us—or maybe they were crickets. It didn't matter. What mattered was, we could hear them.

We felt the breeze in our hair, and smelled the smells of summer—chip trucks, and new-mown hay, and that wonderful, repulsive fishy smell that defines any waterfront anywhere. Smells inaccessible from within a climate-controlled cocoon. I felt myself relaxing and connecting with the world around me. It was a glorious drive.

It was a complete contrast to what I have become accustomed to as driving these days: hurrying to meet some impossible schedule, immersed in traffic for hours at a time; raging at the rampant stupidity that impedes my progress and threatens my life; stressed beyond any reasonable level.

The fact is, the more I have to drive, just to get from place to place, the less I enjoy it—in spite of the fact that driving has long been one of the core pleasures of my life. Don't get me wrong. I still revel in exploring the limits of a fine machine at the track or contemplating the subtleties of its handling on some two-lane twisty. But, like those rides with my dad, that is discretionary driving. Driving I choose to do. Driving that provides its own reward.

The rest is just transportation. And I wonder if there is not a better way. What if, for example, you could simply preset your destination on your car's navigation system, then let it drive itself there, seamlessly dealing with any traffic exigencies along the way, while you read the paper or catch up on your e-mail?

It's an old dream but it is now technically feasible and it is rapidly approaching practical reality. Earlier scenarios involved prohibitively costly roadway infrastructures, but recent developments in the areas of smart cruise control, object recognition, real-time 3D mapping, vehicle-to-vehicle connectivity and other advanced technologies suggest that an Intelligent Transportation System that is primarily vehicle-based is no longer just a dream. It is doable, and it is becoming the natural course of evolution for the automobile.

I won't object when it happens, because it will make those discretionary drives even more special. Then, when twilight approaches, and the cool of the evening moderates the warmth of the wind, and the pressures of the day are behind, I'll invite my sweetheart into the passenger seat, put the top down and our dog in the back, and take a long, slow drive. And I'll enjoy it all the more.

Christopher Black

IT HAPPENED ONE SUMMER

It happened one summer long, long, ago.
I'll tell you the tale before you must go,
A young man's adventure, some claim it was mine,
That took place that summer, in the year '69.

We rumbled on through the Canadian Shield,
Past forest, past lakes, the occasional field,
Like a cinema show on twin lines of steel,
With music supplied by the rhythmic wheel,
As we sat on our heels or stood by the door,
The old with the young and all of us poor.

At the head of the train the red units strained,
To pull all the cars to which they were chained,
Boxcars and flatbeds, tankers, caboose,
"What was that there?" "Oh, that, that's a moose,"
"Say, you from the city, boy, where've you been?"
"Hey, leave him alone. There's things you ain't seen."

They all of them laughed, while some lit a smoke,
And one from the Sault offered all a short toke,
That got us all talking of life, or a love,
And how was sweet Mary knocked up by a dove?
All sorts of questions you can't ask in school,
'Cause questions cause problems and idiots rule.

We slept in our jeans, our shirts and our arms,
Some dreamt of cities, some still of farms,
But all of us dreamt of Vancouver, BC
Where we were headed and all meant to be,
For the buzz on the street said things were cool there,
And even the fuzz would treat you real fair.

But few of us made it, and few of us cared,
The trip was the thing, not how we fared,
For wherever home was, was a place to avoid;
Better the rails than a wife real annoyed,
Or boredom, a bank, or a job you can't find,
Hop a freight once, you'll find your own kind.

Stars that like sequins seemed stitched to the sky,
Lit the star-mirrored lakes like rivers that die,
'Til the morning's new glow outshone them all,
And one boy said "Morning" in a down-easter's drawl,
To which we each answered, this way and that,
Some back to snoring, some up for a chat.

And so the days passed, the train journeyed on,
From the Sault on to Wawa, past White River gone,
On round the lake of Chippewa fame,
The great Gitchigumi, Lightfoot sings of the same;
The wide-open skies directed our way,
'Til on the third day, we hit Thunder Bay.

Most of us hungry, food low in each pack,
We hoped for a shower and time in the sack,
But as the train slowed to crawl through the yards
We knew it was over, we'd played all our cards,

The tracks swarmed with bulls, with cops at their side,
So one jumped, then all, for freedom and pride.

Some made it, some nabbed, with ten days in jail,
Like Lennie the Loop, we couldn't make bail,
So did our short stretch, one day at a time,
Kept ourselves laughing with tall tales of crime,
The guards were okay, at least those in the day,
The night was the problem, with those shadows in play.

They released us real early, and told us to go,
They didn't care where, or even to know,
So we walked a few miles, trying the thumb,
But everyone passed, why pick up a bum,
Yet onward we kept 'til we spotted a train,
Stopped on some tracks all wet from new rain.

"She's headed our way, we'll make Winnipeg,
That's what I reckon, come on, give it some leg"
So lowdown and fast we ran down the line,
Looking for one that seemed to us fine,
Threw our packs in through a wide-open door,
Then jumped in ourselves and rolled on the straw.

We lay back, we laughed, we smelled the cold air,
And wondered if, maybe, this life could be fair,
For happy we were out riding the rails,
For trains on the prairie are ships without sails,
And this one would sail before the moon rose,
For we'd picked this one right, this one that we chose,
To carry us rambling through mountain and field,
Wandering sons of Canada's Shield.

Jennifer Bogart

THE PROMISE

When I watch him sleeping, I wonder how we arrived at this point. I don't yearn for a simpler time, nor do I delude myself into thinking that going back twenty years would do more than allow me to repeat all my mistakes. His even breathing lures me into contemplation. Those blue eyes, hidden by golden-lashed lids, are shielded from the harshness of my reality while holding the secrets of his. Even in sleep, his jaw clenches and restless mutterings disrupt the facade of calm.

I must not love him enough to fulfill my promise.

Outside, the wind shifts direction, and the branches of the old oak sway, coming dangerously close to the window. I had asked him to have the tree trimmed before the winter winds arrived. He'd only smirked and told me there would be time.

"Don't fret so much, Leah," he'd said, his top lip curling into the kind of smile that made me melt. "That old oak was there before us and will continue to stand long after we're gone. The branch can wait."

"Well, when it comes crashing through the window, you'll be the one to clean up the mess." I'd tried hard to resist his charm, but all he'd had to do was tilt his head to the side, allowing the sun to catch his blond highlights amongst the grey, and I found myself falling into his arms and forgetting about the damn tree.

Another gust of wind has me moving to the window. The winter wheat is peeking through the snow, a promise for the spring in the midst of the harsh winter. A dog barks in the distance; I can't see him, but I imagine he is desperate to be inside, where it's safe and warm.

Drake stirs on the bed, fighting his demons, both imaginary and real. I keep reminding myself I only see the shell of who he was, not the person he actually is. I'm fairly certain Drake's essence has long departed from this world and is deeply rooted in an alternate reality—one of his own creation.

This body was not strong enough to contain all that he was. Father, lover, friend—my safe place to land when the world became too much. More than my rock, he was stronger and more consistent than the changing seasons. Just as we know spring will always come to chase away the winter cold, I always knew he would be by my side to help me weather all the storms. I never expected him to lie helpless, beyond my reach, elusive and fragmented. This year, spring won't come for him. He'll drift in eternal winter.

One lonely snowflake rests fleetingly on the window pane. It melts, but is soon replaced with another and then another. I wish they would fill the window like lacy frost, obscuring my view of the world outside. Locking me in; Drake forever by my side.

The first time I met him, I knew we would end up this way. Well, maybe not *this* way, but together until the end of time. He'd been working at Tim Hortons, pouring coffee, dishing up chili, and serving donuts. The ugly brown uniform hadn't detracted from his classic blond looks. At the time, I remember thinking he needed a haircut and then quickly revised my opinion: he was perfect.

"Can I take your order?" He didn't even look up from the cash register as he asked the question.

"I'll have a hot chocolate and a chocolate-chocolate donut, please."

"That's a lot of chocolate."

His comment threw me off. It wasn't his job to judge my order, just take it and serve it. I gave him what I hoped was an even stare, and he broke into an appealing grin, the one that showed off a chipped bottom tooth and deep dimples in his cheeks.

"It comes to two dollars and seventy-six cents. Would you like anything else with that?"

"Well, if this were a fancy café, I'd ask for whipped cream and sprinkles on my hot chocolate...but the usual will have to do."

"I can do that."

"Really?" I returned his smile, feeling my insides starting to twirl.

"Sure. I'm off in about fifteen minutes. Stick around, and I'll whip up my specialty."

"Don't you close in fifteen minutes?" I didn't even know this guy. Despite his overall poster-boy good looks, I wasn't so sure I could trust him. "I uh...I left my cat home alone...I should..."

"Your cat?" He looked skeptical, and I immediately felt the flush of embarrassment creep up my neck and into my cheeks.

"He had surgery." This, at least, was the truth.

"Oh. I hope he's okay."

"Well, it was nothing, really. Just a little snip to render him impo—infertile." I cringed, not liking the way this conversation was going. I was in serious need of a do-over. "Anyway, he'll be fine for a bit, I guess."

In the end, the hot chocolate wasn't anything special, but the company had been spectacular. Now, Tim Hortons happily serves whipped cream on hot chocolate—for a price.

Movement from the bed draws my attention. I should be accustomed to his incoherent mumbles. Weeks have passed since he's uttered anything worth remembering.

Our last conversation had centred on his grandmother's clock. I doubt the timepiece has any real value; it sits on a table in the hallway, refusing to chime on the hour and randomly elicits a cheerful Westminster Abbey when we least expect it. Those bells remind us there are no rules, and the few rules that do exist are meant to be broken.

"You know, my grandmother put a curse on that thing." Drake's smile was weak, but I saw the unmistakable glitter of mischief in his eyes.

I shook my head, refusing to be taken in by his nonsense. "So you keep telling me."

He shifted on the bed, trying to ease the discomfort from hours spent lying in the same position. "She once told me that it only chimes when something memorable is about to happen."

"It didn't chime when Elsie was born."

"How do you know? That was twenty-two years ago, and we weren't home to hear it."

I laughed. "It's just a worn-out keepsake that fills a space on the hallway table."

He grew quiet, his mind drifting into a far-off place I couldn't reach. I squeezed his hand, holding its comfort in mine while he sorted his thoughts. Our conversations were becoming more disjointed as he pulled deeper into his mind, leaving me to flounder outside, waiting and wondering if these would be our last words.

"She loved that clock. Every day, when I was a little boy, she polished it up with her Murphy's Oil, making sure the wood shone and the glass sparkled. It didn't work properly even then. She said that last time she had heard it chime on the hour was when Poppa Norm died…"

I waited. Having heard the story before, I knew he wasn't quite finished telling his tale. A single tear gathered at the corner of his eye and slipped past the edge. His skin used to be golden velvet, the scruff of beard hardly discernible by the end of the day. I watched the tear gather momentum as it rounded the curve of his gaunt cheek and trickled through the bristles of greying stubble before falling unceremoniously onto the collar of his pajamas.

"You don't need to tell me the rest."

He smiled, bringing his eyes to meet mine. His gaze scanned my face, and I thought for a moment he was branding each crevice and crease into his failing memory. "She loved that clock. It reminded her of a time when she was happy, and all was right in her world."

"I know. She was a wonderful woman, your grandmother. I wish I had had the chance to know her better."

"She's calling for me."

I inhaled sharply. I had been warned dementia would start to cloud Drake's ability to reason. The combination of illness and medication made for the perfect recipe of insanity stew. "You're imagining things, Drake. I know you miss her, but—"

"She's calling for me. I can hear her voice whispering in the gears of the clock. Will you bring it to me?"

"What? The clock?"

He nodded, and I could see even that movement was too much for him. Wanting nothing more than to ease his pain and provide him comfort, I agreed. There was no harm in bringing him that old clock.

"You rest. I'll get the clock and set it here, beside your bed."

"Promise?"

"Of course," I said as I left his side to retrieve the clock.

"I want to hear it chime one more time. That's how we'll know."

I stopped at the threshold of the door and turned back to look at him. "I don't understand."

"You made me a promise."

"Yes. I promised to get the clock. I'm getting it now."

"No. The other promise."

I thought for a moment, not wanting to recall the promises I'd made in a more innocent time. Each day melded into the next in a blur of caring for my ailing husband. I bathed him, cooked for him, fed him, medicated him… I had help, but my world revolved around this frail man who lay in the bed, waiting for death to claim his fragile body so his soul could be released into the ether.

The nurse comes into the room, checks his pulse, takes his blood pressure, and taps his IV. I've watched her do it a million times. It's nearly time for lunch, when she'll leave the two of us alone until the night nurse arrives after dinner. Either way, it doesn't matter. I won't leave Drake's side except to shower and use the bathroom unless Elsie is here to sit with him. He needs to be surrounded by family and love, not by strangers paid to do a job.

His breath catches and, for a moment, he struggles. I reach over to grasp his hand in mine, willing him to feel calm and comfortable. This isn't the hand that held mine as we strolled along the shore of Lake Ontario, listening to the gulls and avoiding the frigid water. This isn't the hand that infused me with strength when I laboured with our daughter for thirteen hours. This is the hand of a man whose strength is ebbing, despite my best efforts.

I made a promise, but I don't love him enough to follow through with it. Time and proximity have changed my values, and I can't give him the peace he so desperately needs.

"Leah..." The word is released on a sigh, barely audible between his jagged breaths. "Please..."

Tears well; I can't. The clock on the table chimes the hour, but it's only 11:53.

His lashes part, giving me a glimpse of cloudy blue eyes pleading for release. I close mine, not seeing the dying man in the bed, but the vibrant one I'd made a promise to twenty-five years ago. With his hand in mine, I call on the strength he'd always been so generous to share. Without looking, I key in the code for the IV meds, given to me so I can ease his pain. His lips lift in the beginning of a smile, and he quiets at last.

He was right about one thing—that tree will be there long after we're both gone from this world, but my love for him will last through eternity

Boardwalk after Rain by Reva Nelson

Felicity Sidnell Reid

THE VIEW FROM HERE

New Year, and for a brief moment
there are no strings attached—
it's possible, perhaps, to start
a new life with the midnight clock.
But looking back into the circle
of last year did we look forward
untrammelled by the year before that?
If so, freedom proved illusory,
even resolutions outlived its stay.

But resolve, when called upon,
pushed us through the spiny hedges
on to the gravelled paths of everyday;
a maze of tiny sharpened stones—
those painful, trifling actions or inactions
that fill the long, long days of waiting
Love is swallowed up in taking
care; its object slipping into silence
or sleep, no thought for when or where.

Time and memory have their own duplicity.
Life, the philosopher said, must be lived forward,
but is only understood by looking backward.
On New Year's Day, we drive along
the lake. We sit and contemplate the water,
glutinous and heavy, swaying under cloud.

Then sun leaks through; the lake's grey skin
transfigures. A silver bowl glints
softly, holding out new hope.
We reach for it.

Bill Daniels

JIM

Even though your frame is partially crippled
When I was a kid,
You were one of the big guys on our block
That most looked up to.

I watched.
Amazed at how you played
Road hockey on the avenue.
Perhaps fantasizing that maybe one day…

I went away to find my world.
Persistent memory shadows
Lured me back.

You looked the same, but somehow,
Your voice seemed less tolerant.
They could not taunt you as they once did.
A quick quip brought reverse laughter.

I left again.
Maybe to find a kiln that would mould me.
I still had my boyhood hero.

I was gone longer, then drifted back,
To the village just outside of town.
I was stunned.

That cold snowy day.
Drunk beyond reproach, you staggered
Around the corner of that old decrepit barn,
Axe in a gloveless hand, coat unbuttoned,
No winter boots, an armful of unbalanced kindling.

Your face brightened when you saw me.
Quizzically you probed me.
I was everyone but me.
A boorish taunt bellowed
From inside that old decrepit barn.

You did not respond.
You piled the kindling.
It seemed apathy no longer had an ear.
I watched you chop more kindling,
Then straighten up with a grimace.

I am no longer there.
You are in your world.
Locked in memories that time has clouded.

Listen to the wind, Jim.
It amends memories.
Thrusting them to and fro,
Entombing yesterday.

Rene Schmidt

HOLD THAT WIRE

"Just hold that wire," insisted my oldest brother, Erik. "Nothing will happen, I promise."

He and my other brother, Werner, were working on an old engine our dad had brought home. He wanted us to learn something called *mechanical aptitude*.

"Why should I hold it?"

"We need you to hold it so the engine will start."

"Are you going to shock me?" I asked.

Their faces were creased with sincerity— masks of good intent.

"Honest. We would never do that, would we, Werner?"

"Never."

"Just hold the wire so we can get this thing to work."

"But I'll get shocked…"

"Not if you hold the end of the wire tightly."

"Really?"

"It just can't happen."

"Not at all," agreed Werner.

"Oh, all right." I held the wire for them while Werner knelt and braced the big engine between his legs, staining his tan corduroy pants with engine grease. Erik balanced himself and kicked down on a big kick-start lever with a mighty tromp. A huge blast of electricity jolted through me. I leapt back and hit the wall.

Erik and Werner burst out laughing, "You idiot!" Erik shouted. "Don't you know better than to hold a spark plug wire?"

My aptitude for mechanical things was always worse when my brothers were around. Like when Werner pointed out that my bicycle wheels didn't spin very easily. We had our bicycles upside down doing the maintenance my dad said was useful to learn.

"Spin it and see," he said. I spun the front wheel and after a few turns it stopped.

"Now spin mine." I did and it spun like a top, on and on and on. "You have to loosen the bearings in the wheel hub." He pointed out the slim little nuts in there and left me to it.

"Why's your wheel wobbling like that?" Erik asked a few days later. I was loaded with thirty copies of the *Toronto Star* for my paper route. The front wheel had been turning freely ever since the adjustment. Maybe too freely.

"Werner showed me how to loosen it."

"And you *believed* him?" Erik demanded. "You've got to tighten those," he said, pointing to those nasty thin nuts I had spent an hour on. They were getting more rounded every time I wrenched them with my old adjustable wrench, the only tool I was trusted with. I unloaded the bike, flipped it over, made the adjustment in the growing darkness and took off to deliver the papers. By the time I got back home there was a suspicious grinding sound coming from the wheel hub.

"You listened to Erik? No wonder you screwed it up," observed Werner. "Better do the back wheel now. Even them up."

By the end of the week my bicycle's ball bearings were reduced to some bits of steely gravel and the bearing cups were full of cracks and unusable. Dad was really pissed about me needing two new bicycle wheels.

Things were always breaking down at our house. My dad had loads of mechanical aptitude, which he needed because there was always stuff to fix. Like the night Erik was finally old enough to babysit us. Five minutes after Mom and Dad left Werner began cannonballing onto our old bed, over and over, like a madman. After twenty tries the thing began its death rattle and one end was sagging.

"Werner, you're wrecking the bed!"

"So?" He dived onto it again and it rattled dramatically. "It's fun," he pointed out. The low corner got even lower. He cannonballed into it again. The bed shook like a dog. Another run. This time a belly flop.

"You're wrecking it, stop! Dad'll kill you!" Werner ignored me and belly-flopped onto it again. The footboard collapsed and the steel hooks left deep gouges in the wooden floor.

"Oops!" grinned Werner. I tried to fix the bed with my wrench but couldn't. That night I tried to sleep until our parents got home, but couldn't, in a bed eighteen inches lower at the end, like a ship sinking.

Did I say we were always wrecking stuff? It was either that or chasing each other around the house with something sharp. Mom and Dad never realized that the reason I always went with them was because it was safer than staying home.

For a long time I avoided working on my bicycle and mechanical things in general. Instead I practised shooting my slingshot and learned archery. If they'd offered a course in deadly martial arts for ten-year-olds I would have signed up.

For Christmas Dad bought us a Meccano set with all the little steel brackets and flanges and nuts and bolts, telling us, with pride, how his Meccano windmills and such were used as displays for the toy shop where he grew up in the old country.

"Let's see vat you can make, boysh," he said. My brothers made little racing cars with moving wheels. Dad was disappointed they didn't steer or have a differential. I made a little gallows with a Meccano man hanging from it by his neck. It had no moving parts whatsoever. He shook his head in disgust and said something in Dutch about my mechanical aptitude.

Years later in university I needed a car. I bought a 1967 Volkswagen for $400. It was reliable, free of rust and had been fastidiously maintained by a philosophy grad with a Zen approach to car mechanics. I drove it for two years before my lack of mechanical aptitude confronted me. The car needed an engine job and I couldn't pay a mechanic.

Erik, visiting from out west, was reading on my couch.

"Hey Erik, how about helping me fix the engine?"

"What did your last slave die of?"

"But I don't know how."

"I'm busy," he said, but disappeared and returned, tossing a book on my table: *How to Keep Your Volkswagen Alive: A Manual of Step-By-Step Procedures for the Compleat Idiot*, by John Muir. "This," Erik said, "is all you need to know."

I leafed through it. It detailed every kind of repair for every kind of VW. It had clear drawings of only what you needed to see, and the intro chapter, about people with *no mechanical experience whatsoever*, gave me confidence. The book also had a humorous running commentary about all sorts of other things. I bought some tools and spent the better part of a weekend methodically removing and dismantling my VW engine. I labelled everything, read every paragraph twice and worried constantly. When I had reassembled and put the engine back in there was great apprehension.

"Turn the key," I told myself, but I was afraid of my lack of mechanical aptitude. A voice in my head taunted: "Hold this wire." I walked around the parking lot. I smoked a cigarette. I stared at the car from a distance and hummed a little tune. The key was waiting, dangling in the ignition.

Had I crossed the plug wires?

Had I not attached the gas lines properly?

Would this little car erupt into a fire-bomb and immolate my human remains as a sacrifice to technology?

Finally, my heart beating wildly, I turned the key. There was a pleasant grumble as the four little cylinders fired up and idled happily.

I was ecstatic! Like a new father *I had created life!*

Over the years I did many more jobs on the Volkswagen and even helped friends with their cars. One weekend I was helping Werner wire some speakers into the back of his VW wagon. While he fiddled with the fuses in the front I twisted a wire from his distributor onto the speaker wire.

"You better show me where you want that wire to run," I called.

"Under the trim," he said.

"I can't get it in there."

"It's easy. Just stuff it under."

"I don't want to wreck it. You'd better do it." With a deep sigh Werner extricated himself from under the dashboard and came back to where I held the speaker wire. He stuffed the wire under and I waited until he began attaching it.

"Hey Werner," I said.

"What?" he grunted.

"Hold that wire," I said, turning the ignition key. The audible snap of the high-voltage spark was almost as satisfying as the shocked look on his face.

It took a while to learn mechanical aptitude, but it was worth it.

Shane Joseph

MY LIFE WITH A GUITAR

At a party recently, as alcohol began loosening inhibitions, I was put on the spot in front of a circle of old and newly-made acquaintances. They asked the name of my best and most enduring friend. After swirling the wine in my glass for several seconds, I replied, "My guitar."

Embarrassment engulfed the faces around me. "Not a spouse, or an old school friend, or…or a human?" asked one of the bolder guests.

"No. Just my guitar."

"Not even a dog?"

"No." My certainty caused the circle to disintegrate very quickly thereafter, its members discreetly floating away to join other circles, and I was left mostly to myself for the rest of the evening.

As I drove home later, I tried to figure out why I had been so reckless and made such a politically incorrect declaration. Then my mind went back over the years to the many adventures I had shared with my "best friend"…

***

ACT 1: CHILDHOOD AND THE UKULELE

My first guitar—well, it was a ukulele, actually—came to me when I was sick with the mumps in my native Sri Lanka. My swollen jowls were plastered with a home remedy made of detergent blue and lime that smelled worse than the stinkiest fart. Just one more reason to keep me in isolation. My father pitied me and bought a ukulele. My bachelor uncle, who had once played in a band, taught me the basic three chords so that I could play a ditty with this new instrument. As it was also Christmas (adding to my misery), I first learned to play "Rudolph the Red-Nosed Reindeer." I felt connected to that animal with the prominent facial protrusion—only, his glowed, while mine stank. As the rest of the family shied away from me, I kept company with Rudolph and my ukulele.

Many songs emerged during that lonely Christmas: "Wooden Heart," "Dancing Shoes," "Yarriva!" and bolder ones like "I saw Linda" and "Girls, Girls, Girls," the latter two numbers which I later sang in a concert at my Catholic boys school. Brother Director squirmed in the front seat at this ten-year-old in short trousers and college tie singing liltingly about infidelity and lust. Mother Superior, from our sister girls school, also an invitee to our concert, had a bad attack of coughing throughout my performance.

I soon acquired a reputation as a balladeer and was invited to parties in the neighbourhood where I was given free food and ordered to sing. At one of those parties, a drunken guest thought my ukulele, resting on a chair, was a cushion and sank into it gratefully. When we heard the cracking sound of plywood, we both jumped up, him in the belief that his arse was splintering and me in the knowledge that he had destroyed my pride, joy, and free ticket to unlimited cake and ice cream.

Not to be cowed by this setback, I propped up the collapsed face of my uke with pencil stubs inserted into the belly of the instrument; I glued the back of the uke that had parted company from the rest of the body and tied the base to the neck with string to hold everything together. But my ukulele was like a sinking ship, sucking in air from all openings, old and new, and making my G chord sound like an F flat. Mercifully, as I contemplated burying the poor thing, a burglar broke into our colonial house one night and stole some valuables, including my ailing ukulele. I was heartbroken. This was not how I had wished to see it go.

There is a footnote to this story: the thief was caught when a neighbour reported sounds, comprised of rather flat musical strains, coming from a caretaker's hut in an abandoned construction site. The police raided and caught the burglar singing his lonely heart out while strumming a string instrument held together by…well, string. Our stolen goods were returned, with one exception: my ukulele. Apparently, when apprehended, the thief grabbed at the nearest "weapon" to defend himself. The ukulele splintered into smithereens when the copper hit the robber, sending him and his weapon crashing against the wall of the hut. I refused to accept the remains of my ukulele. I preferred it to be buried a war hero.

***

ACT 2: YOUTH AND THE JUNIOR GUITAR

When I was fourteen, my father won big at the race track. He had bet a DTQQ (Doubles, Triples, Quadruples and Quintuples) on five horses, and won so much money that he went over to the dark side and converted to being a life-long gambler. To celebrate his first win, he splurged on a bicycle for my brother, curtains for the house, dresses for my mother, and a junior guitar for me. Moving up from the four-string ukulele to the six-string guitar was a cinch and added more bass to my earlier tinny renditions. Soon I was back to my former job as neighbourhood entertainer.

At this time, two musical wannabe brothers moved next door with their own guitars but they had a minor problem: they did not know how to play their instruments. They quickly learned from me, however, and we formed a trio named "Bread, Butter and Jam" and set out to make our musical careers. Except a civil war shut down schools and introduced a dusk-to-dawn curfew.

We billed ourselves as "curfew-time entertainers." Our offer was simple: give us enough food (and perhaps a beer or two, for we were now at the stage where we were kissing girls, not merely singing about them) and a place to stay the night, and we would sing from dusk to dawn. At a time when there was no television and the radio played only classical music, interrupted with updates about the government forces beating the rebels, we were welcomed into the neighbourhood homes. We became very popular, and that unhappy time turned into a memorable one.

Of course, success feeds ambition. Very soon we were joined by a drummer, so we became "Bread, Butter, Jam and Marmalade." When two more guys hitched up, we were up to "Bread, Butter, Jam, Marmalade, Bacon and Eggs" and the whole thing was becoming a bit hard to stomach, so we had to abbreviate ourselves down to "Breakfast."

Breakfast had a great run. I remember one gig when we were invited to this rich dude's cabana in the middle of a lake. Ferried over by canoe, we were fed, given the odd beer and asked to sing to this dude's business associates and their wives—a bunch of people who spent their lives at leisure while ancestral inheritances gathered fat interest in their bank accounts.

We had rehearsed for this cabana event with a playbill of songs I kept at my feet to signal the guys what to play next. And we had rehearsed the parts and the harmony, and were nervous as hell. The guests weren't paying us any attention as they were into adult talk, and a lot of drinking. Then the host, a rather corpulent man, clapped his hands and said, "Now boys, earn your dinner, play us a real song from the sixties." In my nervous attempt to please, I kicked the song sheet and it skidded away, slipped between the widely spaced floorboards and fell into the dark waters of the lake. I was gripped with horror; my buddies were looking helplessly at me, and I remembered Brother Director and Mother Superior squirming and coughing. I strummed a G chord on my guitar and said, "Boys, it's 'Girls, Girls, Girls.'" And we belted out Elvis, driven by sheer adrenaline. Our energy caught fire; the adults kicked off their shoes and started dancing. Several songs from Elvis, the Beatles, Tony Orlando and Cliff Richard followed. Chords were misapplied, the harmony was wonky, but who gave a damn—the partygoers were drunk and having a good time! Our first and only set lasted three unbroken hours, until everyone was tired, wasted and looking forward to the *buriyani* dinner that was getting colder by the minute.

The footnote to this story is that the civil war ended, leaving us with the sober realization that the conflict could recur and the country was no longer safe. My band members and their families soon emigrated to Australia, leaving me and my junior guitar behind. It was then I realized who my true pal was, and I played Junior on lonely evenings when dropping in on my departed friends for a jam session was no longer an option. I played Willie Nelson's song "On the Road Again" a lot during that time.

***

ACT 3: ADULTHOOD AND THE CATANIA

I eventually donated Junior to a younger cousin for safekeeping. I wanted my guitar to continue playing even though I was now too big to hold it. I could have sworn that the tone of my Junior had improved in the five years I had owned it, and I got my cousin to swear that he would continue the evolution. There were other guitars that followed but they did not last. They either broke or I gave them away as I could not connect emotionally and musically with them. They were like one-night stands, and I had started to experience those encounters too as I emerged into my twenties.

Then I met the girlfriend who came for twenty-four hours and stayed more than one night, in fact, she shared twenty-four *years* of my life and became my wife. She had a Catania guitar and she did not know how to play. So I would play and sing to her—it became part of my wooing process. When we decided to leave the old country to start a family in a safer place, I went ahead to Dubai to set up base camp. In my possession was a suitcase of clothes, fifty pounds sterling, and the Catania that she knew would keep me company and out of trouble.

That trusty guitar saved my sanity during the months I worked to earn enough money to sponsor my wife. Sharing shabby digs with two other expatriate guys who had unhealthy sleeping and eating habits, I found relief by escaping to the balcony of our poky apartment and playing my guitar, while looking out across the desert to the busy Dubai Creek where the temperature soared above 45 degrees Celsius. I sang "Green, Green Grass of Home" a lot during that time.

My reputation of being not merely an entertainer but a "home entertainment system," something you couldn't buy in the electronics shops littering the emirate, soon spread across Dubai, and I was invited to parties and asked to bring my wife, our kids *and* our Catania. I drank and partied in Dubai more than anywhere else, and this was supposed to be a place that followed strict religious standards! Seven years later, when we left Dubai for Canada, the guys in my office gave me a farewell party with a twist: I was to be the sole provider of the entertainment. The party ran for over five hours and I ended up playing one of my longest never-ending sets until I went hoarse and lost my voice— you might say I worked to the bitter end of my expatriate contract.

They say that immigrants bring the spirit of their ancestors and their traditions, roots and legacies to Canada, making it an inclusive homeland; some even bring their blood-feuds from the old country. All I brought was my family, my savings and my guitar. The Catania served us well during the early, lost months in Canada, especially when the temperature plummeted and we saw snow for the first time in our lives. I played a lot of sad songs during that time and often it was only the Catania that kept me company because my wife and kids were naively shopping and enjoying the novelties of their new homeland my wallet could barely afford. "Blue Eyes Crying in the Rain" was one of my favourites. Rudolph made a brief reappearance, although he had kind of grown up.

But things looked up and career prospects improved and soon, by dint of hard work and never wanting to quit, like that old ukulele, I climbed the corporate ladder to become a jet-setting executive. The Catania lay neglected and began to lose its vibrancy. I did not see the parallel with my own life, for my marriage too was starting to lose its vitality as life paths were diverging in Canada, collateral damage in the immigrant journey. When we separated, my ex took the Catania along with her and with it, the beautiful memories we had shared. I wanted to play Patsy Cline's "I Fall to Pieces" but I didn't have the guitar and that saved me, for I would have slumped into depression. I hope the Catania is still playing somewhere although I cannot hear its tune anymore.

***

ACT 4 (YES, MY STORY HAS A FOURTH ACT!): MY BEST YEARS WITH THE YAMAHA & THE STRATOCASTER

The Yamaha acoustic guitar, bought soon after the collapse of my marriage and perhaps to compensate for it, led to my rebirth. I joined several choral groups that sang to acoustic accompaniment; I sang Italian mountain songs, Sri Lankan folk songs and English pop songs. I began performing at concerts and I started getting paid, in real cash, in addition to the "traditional" currency of food and booze. The Yamaha made me feel like a professional. I learned more chords and trained my voice and now I could play as a rhythm guitarist in a band and sing Neil Diamond in his original key. I enjoyed that period of public performances until a rock band actually came calling and took me on, and that led to the Stratocaster and a further move up the musical stratosphere. I was finally "On the Road Again."

The Fender Stratocaster—my first, and probably my last, real electric guitar—was the guitar of my heroes Jimmy Hendrix and Eric Clapton. My rock band started performing everywhere, from Ontario to British Columbia. And I sang all the songs I had wanted to sing but never had the chance or the backing: Presley, Martin, Santana, Clapton, Kristofferson, Humperdinck, Sinatra—I did it all, my way. But we had a challenge: our band members would change frequently as their lives and day jobs evolved. And we all needed a day job, because cover bands, like most artists in Canada, don't earn a living wage. And with every change our sound altered, the dynamics and politics deepened and the practice sessions between gigs increased. There were times when I was happy with my band and other times when I was in conflict with some of its members. The gigs started getting complex and demanding and I had to keep reminding myself that this was a hobby, not an occupation, although sometimes it felt like the latter.

But the band and my guitar also saved my sanity when my jet-setting business career finally ended, like corporate careers do when aging executives are put out to pasture in Canada. I was given a golden parachute and offered time to write my memoirs. How does one compensate for the loss of purpose and identity that a career bestows? I embraced the music to fill the void, and it did not disappoint me. More gigs, more songs, more practices and long, tiring drives followed.

Then a band member died of a heart attack, two others divorced, and finding replacements became a gnawing headache.

And our songs were starting to get outdated. A couple of years into this unsettled period and we reached the inevitable conclusion: our road was fast approaching its end. Then one cold and dark morning, after a gig the night before, and after hauling equipment back to our storage space and driving from the west end of Toronto to my new home in Cobourg, I fell asleep at the wheel of my car and went through two stop signs before waking up to realize that God had given me another chance and shown me a sign that the end had arrived. We disbanded.

I re-invented myself a final time and gave solo musical performances to bolster my writing career, which had started to take off—after all, I had much to write about now. I found that music and literature were good bedfellows. If I gave a prose reading and coupled it with a few songs, I was sure to sell more books than usual, to any audience. And they would remember me as—"Oh you're the author who sings and plays guitar!"

Now, as the twilight deepens and my fingers stiffen and refuse to fly over the fret board like they once did, I gaze upon my guitars reposing in their sturdy cases, and reflect upon them and their predecessors, and I relive all of life's milestones that the various iterations of this instrument have accompanied me through, making the harder passages bearable, the happier ones joyous, and lending colour and depth to them all. And I think of Matt Monro's rendition of "The Impossible Dream":

"…That one man, scorned and covered with scars,
Still strove with his last ounce of courage,
To reach the unreachable star…"

***

ENCORE:

I recently bought my one-year-old grandson a ukulele…

Reva Nelson

MY BEST FRIEND LAURA

I first met Laura in 1960; I hadn't really heard of her before then. I was eleven years old, in Grade 8, at Memorial Public School in Hamilton, Ontario. Steeltown. Where you grow up breathing in iron filings from Stelco and Defasco and there are dead silvery fish floating in the lake and baking on the beach but no one calls it pollution. We fling the fish at each other for fun. That's Hamilton.

My life was the same as most everyone else's at that time. We had a Dodge car and a Westinghouse fridge and my mom stayed home to make us Campbell's tomato soup with Saltine crackers for lunch. My guess is that everyone else on the street had that same lunch most days. I think I was sort of smart because I skipped Grade 3, along with Susan Whittaker who was a big, stocky girl, Candice McPherson who was petite and cute and George Nickerson who came from England and wore short pants.

Our English teacher was a short, mean tyrant who made us study poems and recite them from memory. We had to write our own speeches and then stand up in front of the whole class to deliver them. She could make anyone quiver with just one glance. Even the biggest boys, who towered sky-high above her head, were afraid of her. I was shy beyond measure and scared to death.

There was going to be a speaking contest. We all had to prepare a special speech for it, longer than anything we'd done so far. Miss Wingrove called us up one by one to discuss our topics. She suggested a strong female for me to talk about. I didn't know of any. No one talked about any females then, weak, strong or otherwise. In school we learned about the men who made our country and invaded other ones. Females were homemakers or teachers or the Queen. We sang to Her Majesty every morning but no one ever said what she accomplished. My friend's mother got a job in a dress shop; that was revolutionary.

Then my mean teacher asked if I'd ever heard of Laura Secord. Of course I had. She made chocolates and had some stores. This was pre-Internet and Google days and I had no idea she was a heroine of some sort. My teacher suggested that I ask my mother to take me to the library to get a book about Laura Secord. That became the day I fell in love.

This was all pre-Canadian history moments on TV, pre-Canada proud, pre-feminism or female power of any kind (that we knew of; I don't think we ever heard of Nellie McClung or the suffragettes), pre-female role models, pre-learning of much Canadian history at all, and post American and British history in school.

That day, in the Hamilton library, the day I fell in love, I discovered Laura Secord, the heroine of the War of 1812. She was magnificent! Forget about Superman and Batman. I now had a Superwoman in my life.

When Laura Secord was home, nursing her husband who had been wounded at Queenston Heights, she overheard the Americans' plans for a surprise attack on the British. She stole away early in the morning and marched through the woods for twenty miles, with her cow, to warn Lieutenant FitzGibbon about the impending attack. The information she shared helped the British and their Mohawk warrior allies to stop the invading Americans at the Battle of Beaver Dams. Some say the story may not be true, especially about the cow, but I believed in Laura for sure. She wouldn't lie about something so scary. It was 1813 and I don't think anyone would pretend something so grand.

Not only that, when I delivered my speech about my new friend Laura, my classmates listened. I got the highest marks of any presentation. I did a good job talking about that Laura. Then I was chosen to speak at the Hamilton YMCA on Ottawa Street in the contest sponsored by The Canadian Legion. This was a big deal. I was so scared.

That next week, something else amazing happened. My teacher, that tiny demon named Miss Wingrove, became nice. She changed before my eyes. She helped me learn my speech and deliver it perfectly. She taught me that the hard *g* at the end of a sentence, the way my immigrant father spoke, was not pronounced as a *guh* in Canada. So not "walking-guh," but "walking," with a soft *g*. We practised every lunchtime for two weeks. She was so helpful and so encouraging and kind that I could scarcely believe it. Finally the newly transformed Miss Wingrove said I was ready.

I was terrified

Unlike Laura, I had no flanks of a cow to hide behind. I thought I was going to go up in a tornado of smoke when my turn to speak came. I could barely breathe. My knees were shaking so badly that my skirt was moving in the breeze. I felt that everyone could tell. I looked out at Miss Wingrove and she was smiling at me. Smiling!

I gulped like a guppy on the line, then started to talk about my new pal, Laura Secord. Everyone's eyes were on me. I just thought about Laura and told her story. If she could do it, so could I. I grabbed onto her bravery, and I got people to laugh at the cow part. They clapped. The judges deliberated for what felt like a very, very long time. And then I won.

I was handed a large white envelope with a letter of congratulations and a five-dollar bill. In those days, that was a terrific amount of money. I couldn't believe it.

The very next day, I took the bus downtown with my new best friend, Laura. We bought a new pencil case, a Paul Anka record and of course, some Laura Secord chocolates.

We had a wonderful time.

Susan Statham

THE REVENANT

The research, planning and execution had taken her forty days, but in just forty minutes she would learn the measure of her success. She inhaled deeply, exhaled slowly. All would be well, she told herself.

Paintings are an extension of the artist and for Agnes, her portraits were like multi-coloured offspring who, after weeks of doting care, were sold into captivity. And as an artist who lived to work but also worked to live, she was familiar with the melting pot of emotions that accompanied the sale of each canvas-baby: excitement, anxiety, gratitude and regret.

Ben, her neighbour, stepped from his apartment just as Agnes locked her door. "Hey, thanks again for dinner last night." He pointed at the folded rectangle of cardboard leaning against the wall. "Is your painting in there?"

"Yes. I had to use this packaging a framer gave me because the painting's too big for any of my portfolios. Not very professional looking, but it'll only fit between the front and back seats of my car, and it needs some protection."

"It'll work." He took a closer look. "I see it's even got a handle."

Agnes struggled to raise the corners of her lips.

"Don't look so worried. The portrait's the most important thing, and you did a stellar job. He's like a revenant."

"A what?"

"Someone you brought back from the dead."

Her face involuntarily puckered. "Eww."

"But in a good way," said Ben. "In fact, we had a chat last night."

"Who's we?"

"Your masterpiece and I—while you were in the kitchen getting dessert, I went into your studio."

Agnes eyed him suspiciously.

"I just wanted one more look, but next thing you know I'm asking him about the birth of our country, life as a Canadian prime minister and if that collar is as uncomfortable as it looks."

Agnes admitted she sometimes talked to her subjects. "But the important question is, did he answer you?"

Ben gave her a look of disdain. "Of course not." His face softened. "But I think he really wanted to."

She joined in his laughter. "Thanks, I needed that." As Agnes stepped into the elevator and before the door slid closed, she heard him call out, "I want to hear all about it when you get back."

While driving to the gallery, Agnes imagined possible scenarios. Her favourite was the "awed jaw-drop," but she'd be almost as happy with a congratulatory handshake or "Excellent work, Miss Lamont"; even a dismissive "Yes, very good" would be better than any version of "this is not acceptable." But at her most imaginative, Agnes could not have conjured up what actually happened.

On schedule and a few minutes before the five o'clock closing time, Agnes pulled into the parking lot. The cardboard portfolio with its precious cargo didn't slide out of the car quite as easily as it slid in, but she managed with a little wrangling and carried it safely up the stairs and into the main part of the gallery.

"Hello Agnes," said Leslie, the gallery manager. "Mr. Smith is upstairs. I'll just let him know you're here."

She looked around for a spot to display the painting. "Do you have an empty easel?" Agnes asked before realizing she was alone in the room. "I'll take that as a no," she muttered and opened the portfolio to remove the painting. She chose to lean it against one of the pillars and in the best light rather than where it would be visible for Smith as he descended the staircase.

When he entered the room his greeting was not without warmth, but he quickly turned his attention to the canvas and said…nothing, for a full agonizing minute. Then he smacked his hands together with a cheery "Right" and invited Agnes to join them for dinner.

"It's Italian, the food is excellent," he said.

Agnes, having momentarily forgotten what she was wearing, glanced down quickly to reassure herself it was suitable for fine dining. Smith added that it would give them an opportunity to talk about the painting and the project.

This has positive possibilities, thought Agnes, and accepted the invitation.

"Leslie will lock up and meet us there," said Smith. "It's the Cibus, do you know it?"

"Cibus? Unusual name," she said.

"I believe it's Latin for food. I can't recall the address, but it's on Elgin. Did you drive?" When she nodded, he suggested she simply follow him. Then he reached down and scooped up the canvas. "I'll take this with me."

She walked with him to the exit before remembering the portfolio and ran back for it. In the parking lot Agnes watched the gallery owner putting the unprotected canvas into his trunk.

She approached him with the battered cardboard. "I got this from a friend, she's a framer, because I didn't have a portfolio big enough. Would you like to use it to, um, protect the painting?"

"No. It'll be fine," he said and as he passed his foot under the rear bumper the trunk lid gently closed.

Well I guess it will, thought Agnes.

En route to her car the wind caught what now felt like a cardboard sail threatening to blow her off course and slowing her departure. She was relieved to see Smith waiting at the exit, but he promptly slipped into traffic as she approached. Feeling like a cop tailing a suspect, Agnes sped into the lane, cringing when a motorist blasted his horn but relieved to keep the black BMW in her sights. Fifteen minutes later she found one of the few empty parking spots and climbed from her car. Smith waved her toward the side door of the restaurant.

As they entered, Agnes marvelled at the mosaic floor tiles, the Tuscan columns dividing the spacious dining area and the warm smell of roasted garlic. Smith waved at a small group seated around a large, linen-draped table. "We're meeting a few of my friends."

Eschewing the chair at the head of the table Smith sat between a dark-haired woman of indeterminate age and a balding man with an expertly trimmed beard. Smith motioned for Agnes to choose one of the remaining seats. Across the table an older woman smiled pleasantly and tapped the chair to her left. "Sit here, dear." And when Agnes joined her she added, "I'm Marie."

This prompted Smith to begin introductions. "Agnes, this is Chandra." But he was interrupted by Leslie's arrival so the bearded man remained nameless.

Like a hummingbird, the waiter, bearing the name François on his name tag, flitted to each guest delivering menus. Smith suggested a favoured Italian red wine and it was promptly delivered and poured. He raised his glass. "To the success of a new venture."

Leslie told Agnes they were opening an art supply store next to the gallery and with a nod toward the bearded man added. "Raymond works for a major supplier, and his wife Chandra, with Marie's help, will manage the store."

Before she could ask when the store would open Smith said, "Did I mention that Agnes is an artist?"

All faces turned in her direction. "What kind of art do you do?" asked Marie.

Pushing back his chair, Smith stood, raised his right hand to signal a prompt return and left the restaurant. While they waited, the menus were read and comments popped up like the little bubbling mud pots of Yellowstone Park.

Within a few minutes, Smith returned carrying the canvas and for a moment he paused in indecision. Abruptly, he pulled out the chair at the head of the table and seated the painting to face the group. "This is part of a project to celebrate Canada's one-hundred-and-fiftieth birthday, and Agnes is the artist."

She was pleased to hear pleasure in his voice and though the gathering didn't burst into spontaneous applause, Agnes felt approval in their nods and smiles. She was asked about the composition, the meaning of the painting within the painting and how she achieved such luminosity in the flesh.

"I heard he's a favourite of our present prime minister," said Leslie.

Marie leaned closer to the painting. "Ah, the stories this man could tell. He was one of Canada's best loved prime ministers. Did you know that?" she asked Agnes, who nodded. "Of course you did. I can see a lot of research went into this. I bet you didn't know Lucy Maud Montgomery thought he was almost perfect. 'Just a little lower than the angels' is how she described him."

"I know he won four consecutive majority governments and during those fifteen years, Canada got another railroad, two more provinces and the navy." Agnes's enthusiasm suppressed her natural shyness. She was ready to tell the "sunny way" story when François reappeared to take their orders.

Jotting down each request, he turned toward the head of the table, paused, looked to the group, then again to the painting. "Wow, that's something you don't see every day." Agnes watched him walk to the kitchen, but within a minute he was back and he wasn't alone.

"Good evening, I'm Guido, your chef and the owner of Cibus. François tells me there is someone here I must see." He took his time studying the canvas. "And the artist, he is here?"

Smith gestured toward Agnes. "Yes she is. This is Agnes Lamont."

"I am Italiano; I know art." Guido's chest expanded beneath his apron. "You do fine work, Miss Lamont." He bowed and kissed her hand. "Now I go to the kitchen and for you, I do fine work too." He was true to his word and fine meals were enjoyed by all.

When Agnes returned to her apartment, Ben was sitting in the hall reading a book. Seeing her, he pushed himself to his feet. "Agnes! Did everything go okay? What took you so long?"

"I was having dinner with Sir Wilfrid Laurier."

Marie-Lynn Hammond

THE BRIDGE

When I was growing up, only one bridge spanned the Ottawa River between Ottawa and Hull: the Interprovincial Bridge. I can remember a time when the Ontario side of the bridge was paved and the Quebec side wasn't. When you saw the sign halfway across saying "*Bienvenu au Québec*" and your car wheels hit those wooden planks, you *knew* something had changed.

Two separate cities, inextricably linked. You couldn't live in one without being aware of the other. As I remember it, it was like this: Ottawa was English, Protestant, rich, and staid. Hull was French, Catholic, poor, and funky. It was where all the Ottawa university students went to party. The bars stayed open later, the drinking age was younger, you could buy beer at a grocery store, and the French girls were—well, they were *French.* And everyone knew what that meant.

For me, though, the differences weren't quite so clear-cut. Although my mother's family was French and her parents had been born in Quebec, they had emigrated to Northern Ontario. In the 1930s they and their large brood settled in the Ottawa-Hull region, and there they stayed, living largely in French but able to get by in English. Most lived on the Ontario side, but there was a certain amount of to-ing and fro-ing across the river. And then my mother had the daring to marry an English Canadian, so I was a hybrid, who spoke both French and English.

In 1965 my family was living in North Bay, and I'd been accepted to Carleton University in Ottawa for the fall. Normally I'd have spent the summer at our cottage on Lac Simon north of

Montebello, but the year before, after intense parental resistance, I'd acquired a horse. The deal was, if I won a scholarship, I could take him to college. If not, I'd have to sell him. I won the scholarship.

We found a place to board Traveller on the Aylmer Road, on the Quebec side, where everything seemed to be cheaper, and that summer I was sent to stay with one of my mother's brothers, Mistai Vaillant, and his wife, Lucille. They owned a little grocery store in Hull and were delighted to host me; they loved children but had none of their own.

It was an idyllic time. In the morning I'd catch the Aylmer bus to the farm where Traveller was stabled and spend the day riding through sun-bleached fields and shaded woods. There were mansions along the Aylmer Road that fronted onto the river, and I noticed that most of the names on the mailboxes were English. The stable owners and horse owners in the area were also Anglo. The stable hands at the farm, though, were French.

I suppose I was already aware that the English, with their power and money, felt contempt for French Canadians, whom they tended to view as illiterate peasants. I know that, away from my mother's family, I unconsciously played down my francophone side, an easy thing to do with my father's Anglo name and my unaccented English. But I didn't stop to analyze. What did politics matter, anyway, to a seventeen-year-old living out her equine passions in that shimmering green-and-gold summer?

In the late afternoon, I'd head back from the stables to my aunt and uncle's place and start the vegetables for supper. Mistai and Lucille lived behind their store in a tiny, old-fashioned apartment, which consisted of a large kitchen and a bathroom on the ground floor, and one upstairs room partitioned to form two small sleeping spaces. There was no living room or dining room. But then, my aunt and uncle practically lived in the store, which they always kept open later than the brash new supermarkets—the only way they could compete.

I loved that little store, with its rickety screen door and creaky wooden floors and faded cut-outs on the walls of pretty girls drinking Coca-Cola. After supper I'd hang around the cash register, drinking cream soda and chatting in French to my aunt, while my transistor radio played the hit parade, in English, in the background. It was pleasant, but part of me was just a little lonely.

One night a boy walked into the store. We stared in surprise at each other. It turned out we'd met once before, up at the lake the previous summer. Michel, who lived in Hull, was French, although his English was quite good. He was two grades behind me and a whole year younger, but something about his shiny dark hair and soulful brown eyes made me feel I could overlook this. We began to go for long walks. Mostly we spoke French. He was the first francophone boyfriend I'd ever had, and I discovered something. In French, you could talk about the most serious, heartfelt, emotional stuff and it didn't sound corny. It sounded wonderful—and *right.* Somewhere in the middle of our second conversation, I fell in love.

After I met Michel, the days flew by. During those long summer evenings we walked and talked and poured our hearts out. Sometimes he recited French poetry to me, and sometimes, in the shadow of the maples behind the store, we kissed. Then suddenly it was September, and time for me to start a new life as a college student in residence.

"*C'est pas loin,*" he would say, pointing across the river to Ottawa. "*On se reverra certainement.*"

I wanted to believe him, believe we'd see each other again. The river divided, but, as I knew, things weren't black and white. There was also the bridge. Surely the bridge connected?

I settled into residence and started university. I was unprepared for the busyness and confusion of it all. Registration, freshman initiation, lectures and meetings and parties and—dates. It's not that I'd forgotten Michel, but all of a sudden guys were asking me out, something that had never happened in high school. Meanwhile Michel was trying to reach me by phone, but I was rarely in the dorm. When I'd finally phone back, I'd get his mother. The one Saturday I was able to make it across the Interprovincial Bridge by bus, he was at his great-uncle's funeral forty kilometres away. So I rode my horse through the crisp autumn woods and tried to recall the exact shade of Michel's eyes

Finally, three weeks after parting, we managed to reach one another. Already his voice on the telephone sounded wistful, distant, and—dare I say it—foreign. Still, we agreed to meet the next Saturday, in the residence lounge.

When I came down to meet him, he was standing stiffly by the lounge door, wearing a suit. I was taken aback. I'd never seen him in a suit before.

"Hello," he said, shy and almost formal. "It's great to see you again."

This was the second surprise. He was speaking English, and in English, he sounded the way he looked: awkward, uncomfortable. The soulfulness and poetry was gone, crowded out by the hard consonants and unmusical vowels of that other language.

Looking back, I understand it now. He was in alien territory. Around us, knots of confident students were laughing and calling out—in English. So why didn't I have the courage to shift to French? I suppose I too felt intimidated. Instead, I became tongue-tied, in both languages.

We muddled through for almost an hour, and then he looked at his watch. We both knew it was over.

"I must go now," he said. "Goodbye."

We shook hands like strangers, then impulsively he leaned over and kissed my cheek. I started to draw back, but he moved in again, and suddenly I remembered. Of course! In Quebec, you kiss *both* cheeks. I mumbled an apology, my face burning, and moved forward again to complete the stilted little embrace.

As his lips brushed my face, he murmured, "*Au revoir*, Marie-Lynn," and he walked away. I wanted to cry out, "Wait, Michel, come back!" but I couldn't think of the French words. They were gone too. And I knew it wouldn't work in English. So instead I stood there and watched him disappear.

Now, I wonder, how did he feel, on the long ride back down Bronson Avenue, back to the other bus at the city's edge, the one that would take him over the bridge and across the river? As for me, I wasn't feeling anything. I didn't want to. There was a bridge inside me, and I'd just knocked it out. It would be years before I would feel ready to face the other side of the river—and rebuild once again.

Illustration by Pegi Eyers

Pegi Eyers

MY HOME ON NATIVE LAND

When our ancestors arrived on the shores of Turtle Island, they brought their cultural beliefs and social mores with them. They were looking for a fresh start, but instead of taking their cues from the indigenous civilizations already thriving in the "new world," they replicated the familiar lifeways of home and went on to repeat the colonial pattern.

As we fast forward to the present, in my work as a social justice activist I am often asked if things could have been different in the beginning, in our "first contact" interactions with First Nations. But I honestly don't think we can just imagine a kinder, more benevolent settler society into being. The mad scrabble to build Empire and grab land, resources, title, and prestige were the priorities of the day, and other than as trading partners and wilderness guides, First Nations had little place in that rosy picture.

However, as the settlement of what was to become Canada progressed, miracles were happening. When a Scottish family with a newborn baby wound their way through southern Ontario in 1832 by coach and Durham boat, their craft capsized in the waters known today as the Narrows at Lake Couchiching. The tiny baby was my third great-grandmother, Eliza Emily Bailey, and she was rescued from the channel and brought safely to shore by a kind member of the Chippewa (Ojibway) Nation. As part of the immigrant wave that engulfed a pristine wilderness, the flourishing of my ancestors has given me the haunting legacy of her miraculous rescue and my deep roots in the Ontario landscape. Seven generations later, I am astonished at how this story transcends ordinary ethnoautobiography, and am overcome by a series of questions tangled up with destiny, kindness, reciprocity, retribution, ancestral memory, and structural inequality.

First of all, I wonder about the obvious: would the generations of my family line even exist had Eliza perished in the waters of Lake Couchiching? Would musical icon Gordon Lightfoot (my uncle and direct descendant of Eliza Bailey) have been born and gone on to write a canon of songs that defined the narratives of Canadian nationalism and celebrated Canadian identity? And who was her rescuer exactly, and was he thanked profusely for his service? The story may be dramatic but it is far from unique, as countless narratives describe how the "first contact" settler society was welcomed and dependent upon First Nations everywhere, who freely gave us gifts of food, land, medicine, and our very lives. The trail is cold, but their original generosity and kindness is deeply woven into the heritage fabric of our families and communities. Even the structure of Canada owes a great collective debt to the first peaceful treaty agreements between Indigenous and non-Indigenous leaders, and to the partnership model of Indigenous diplomacy that contributed to our first constitutions and laws.

Canada's first constitutional document, the 1763 Royal Proclamation, was ratified in 1764 at the Treaty of Niagara between the British and two thousand leaders from the First Nations surrounding the Great Lakes—the Nipissing, Anishnaabe, Algonquin, Odawa, Huron, and Haudenosaunee. At this event, the British accepted a nation-to-nation relationship rooted in a policy of non-interference, and codified by the symbols of covenant chains and wampum belts in sacred ceremony. All parties agreed to benefit equally from the bounty of the land. The ongoing legitimacy of Canada, and our Canadian identity, stems from these original constitutional relationships between the settler society and First Nations. Rooted in the philosophy and practice of non-interference, peaceful co-existence, and respect, the founding agreements make us all treaty people, and the legacy of Indigenous diplomacy, law, and peacemaking benefit all Canadians. The ensuing years of oppression, archaic legislation such as the Indian Act, and domination over Canada's First Nations does not detract from the foundational status of the treaties.

Like so many others in the Americas, my family owes our lives to First Nations, but what have we done to return the favour? In stark contrast to the success of Eliza Emily Bailey and her descendants, what has been the experience of the Ojibway people since 1832? They have suffered loss of their lands, oppression, assimilation, residential schools, and relocation. And how do we reconcile the kindness our ancestors received with the stereotypes of "primitive" that enabled this harsh treatment? Growing up in our secure and happy world here in Ontario, did we see that First Nations were living like second-class citizens? Or did we take the time to recognize the beauty and diversity of the cultures that had lived in the area for millennia?

In my case, with a major shift from the political to the personal, how was I supposed to integrate the new information about Eliza Emily Bailey into my contemporary life? I had been drawn to learning about First Nations culture and history for many years, and at the exact moment that I discovered the story of her miraculous rescue, I was already involved with social justice activism in solidarity with Indigenous people. Connecting directly with an ancestor is not an easy thing to do, but was I responding to Eliza's directive on some deep level, to give back to the First Nations who had given so much to me? Today, my focus on First Nations solidarity work has increased far beyond what I ever would have imagined.

In the interest of being a good ancestor to the next generation, I have come to the conclusion that my purpose is to engage with the truth, challenge the racism found in mainstream society, and create much-needed space for healing and reconciliation. The struggle for all descendants of the original settler society must be to shift from unconscious denial and guilt about our colonial legacy to the righteous anger of critical thinking, reflection and social activism. And as we come to an authentic recognition of our shared history with First Nations and explore the myths and misconceptions we have about each other, we can become empowered to use our new-found awareness to build solidarity and use it as a catalyst for change.

There is much we can do to eliminate institutional racism and contribute as allies to the anti-oppression, human rights, and land claims struggles of our First Nations neighbours. The hope for social justice and a new, sustainable society will be built on egalitarian values that embrace all forms of difference—all colours, all ethnicities, and all religions. Right now, learning intercultural competency skills, respecting Indigenous cultures and lifeways, attending anti-racist trainings, and understanding white privilege from reading or videos is our first step.

As I hold the story of Eliza's rescue deep in my heart, my eternal gratitude for her rescuer is rooted in the no-time and no-place of the spirit world. And in the end, the interface of my own family with the Anishnaabe people leads me to believe that as we shake free of our colonial past, it is essential that we all become protectors of Turtle Island, to stop the destruction and plunder of what have become our ancestral lands as well. As we celebrate the privileges and amenities of this great country, Canada, it may be a good idea to finally become intimate with "place." Not as a backdrop to our daily round, or as landscapes to enjoy, or sites for managed spaces like gardens, but as lands of the greatest beauty that have their own right to life and that hold all the elements we need to thrive, and also as sites of unimaginable destructive power that are wild and unknowable, that have their own purpose and trajectory, that are held sacred, and that are beloved by countless diverse groups of Indigenous peoples.

Can we also, before it is too late, dedicate ourselves to that love? By virtue of our rootedness in our communities, our buried ancestors, and our mutual regard for the land, for better or worse both Indigenous and non-Indigenous people now share Turtle Island, and it may not be too late to establish the peaceful co-existence that the colonial powers denied us all.

Diane Taylor

AN IRISH LAMENT

I'm Irish. That's the short story. My father's parents were born in the small seaport town of Sligo, on the west coast of Ireland. I never knew them; they both died before I was born. In fact, Dad doesn't remember his mother because she died when he was just three—of peritonitis from infection after an appendectomy here in Canada. His distraught father swore he'd murder the surgeon. Then at sixteen, his father died. At sixteen, my father was at the mercy of his own wits…of which he had plenty.

Black wavy hair and bright blue eyes, large wobbly ears and large knuckled hands, Dad had a way with words. He always won the Scrabble games. He recited Tennyson and Robbie Burns at length. When I complained about a teacher, he cautioned me: "Learn in spite of the teacher." When I dedicated my first book to my mother (who was overjoyed for days), I was worried Dad would be jealous, but he said, while shaving one morning, "Never miss the opportunity to make someone happy." After my divorce, I was a very sad young woman. What can a father do? He sent me a letter that contained three words: "I love you." That letter is over fifty years old now, tucked away in my jewellery box.

And there's the time Dad and I were visiting my friend Carol in the wilds of rural Florida, near the Everglades. (You should see the size and speed of the spiders let alone the alligators.) One night we were wakened by loud crashing noises in the brush outside the house. Carol ran quietly in bare feet from her bedroom and whispered that there'd been a lot of break-ins lately. What to do? How to defend ourselves? The Doberman panted and trembled.

Dad ran noisily from the couch in the living room, slammed a door and shouted, "Harry! Get the gun! Get the gun!" Harry? Gun? You have to hand it to my dad.

At some point, as a young adult, I began to miss having grandparents—that path back and back. There was no one to call "Grandpa"—not on my mother's side, either, for he died before I had a chance to meet him. And her mother died while still in her twenties when Mom was five. In the absence of living ancestors, I longed for connection with my forebears dead and buried.

I felt the absence as a presence. It accompanied me like a melody droning in the distance, like an Irish lament moaning across the ocean. I needed psychic connection to those from whom I was descended. What were their dreams, their struggles? Were they farmers, shoemakers, midwives, poets? What was life like in Ireland? Why did they come to Canada? What were their stories? How would I feel by catching glimpses of them?

Therefore, in my mid-forties, I recorded an oral history of my father's memories of stories he remembered of and from his father. We met twice a week for a month.

At the time, I was a French teacher, indulging my fascination with language. So it was with great astonishment and delight when Dad told me how, when his aunts and uncles came to visit in Brantford, Ontario, they would start talking in English. Then the English would get "very broad." Then, when they reminisced about Ireland they would get excited and it would become pure Gaelic. "*Gaelic!*" I almost shouted. "Yes," he said. "They probably spoke Gaelic at home and in the streets, and learned English at school." Just knowing that left me breathless—though Gaelic itself opened up another mystery. Soon after, I took classes in conversational Gaelic. But no matter how hard I tried, Gaelic would remain a mystery. Still, I am fiercely proud of my wild linguistic roots.

***

In 1984, I recorded my father talking about his memories of his own father—my grandfather. Here are some of those oral histories:

"In Ireland, my dad played football [what we call soccer] and hurling, which is a vicious game played with a stick and a ball that is smaller than a lacrosse ball. The main idea, of course, was to go after the ball, but Uncle Harry would say that it wasn't a real game unless you forgot the ball and went after somebody's head.

"My mother, Annie Sheeran, was a singer back in Ireland. She sang with John McCormack before he became famous and made hundreds of records. My dad had some of his records and my brothers and I listened to them over and over.

"My dad didn't ride horses as far as I know. The main means of transportation in Ireland was bicycles and jaunting cars. These latter were two-wheeled carts drawn by a pony or donkey.

"I never heard my dad talk about going to the pubs in Ireland, I guess because it cost money and they wouldn't have had much. The economic conditions there were one of the reasons for coming to Canada. Memory of the famine was still recent.

"When my dad and Uncle Harry and Uncle Joe and Aunt Liza got together, they would reminisce about life back in Ireland. Good stories! Sometimes, at night, they would go out and steal a sheep."

Astonished, I asked, "What for?"

"To eat," he said, in a tone of voice that implied, "What else?"

"Well, who from," I asked, my mind still boggled.

He was laughing and said, as if it was a silly question, "From somebody who had them. One night, my dad and Uncle Harry and a third person got together and told this story, and I heard it many times after that so I guess it's true. They'd been biking around during the day and had seen some sheep on a farmer's land, and they went back that night on bicycles to get one. The way they always did it was to stun the sheep with a pick handle and then drag it away. So this dark and moonless night, they went back to the spot and came to the stone wall that surrounded the field. They parked the bikes and climbed over, and a bit beyond, they saw this white shape lying on the ground. Aha! A sheep! Uncle Harry swatted it with the pick handle and the thing rose up in front of them like a huge ghost. It was a big white horse."

Dad is laughing one of his almost uncontrollable laughs.

"It put the fear of God into them, and they turned and ran, blind with terror, and ran right into the stone wall. They were going so fast that their bodies flipped right over the wall, and they kept on running."

Dad is laughing and laughing.

"They'd have been eighteen or nineteen at the time, and there were many times when they went to bed hungry."

Tears of laughter are in danger of turning into something else, but Dad is adept at turning the conversation around.

***

Progressing into my dad's past gave me a deeper understanding of my father, of myself, and of an era. Bringing departed ancestors into my life expanded me. I walk accompanied by ancestral music and ancient wisdom—glimpses of, at any rate. I walk accompanied.

To quote the gifted First Nations writer Richard Wagamese who, I'm sorry to say, died earlier this year, "We are story. All of us. What comes to matter then is the creation of the best possible story we can while we're here; you, me, us, together. When we can do that and we take the time to share those stories with each other, we get bigger inside, we each see other, we recognize our kinship—we change the world, one story at a time…"

Patricia Calder

ROOTS

After his final submission to the *Huntley Herald*, Darcy raced the five miles out of town in his pickup and peeled into the shed at the farm. His great uncle Callum had the Volvo hood propped up. The old man must be working on the station wagon again. Darcy jumped out of the pickup and headed up the steps to the mudroom when a noise caught his attention.

"Uncle Callum?" Darcy stepped back down the stairs and around the station wagon. A pair of legs in overalls protruded from under the vehicle. Darcy ran to his side and squatted. "Hey," he shouted, bending to peer at his great uncle in the darkness.

The old man groaned an unintelligible answer.

Darcy considered phoning his mother, but dialed 911 instead.

Later, in the Huntley Hospital, Darcy was hanging out in the waiting room. His mind raced with questions. If Uncle Callum died, who would inherit the farm? If Uncle Callum didn't die, should he tell his mother about the heart attack? What about the dog? How long would Uncle Callum be stuck in hospital? How long would Darcy have free run of the farmhouse?

Darcy had only been working for the *Huntley Herald* a few months. It would have been impossible for him to live at home so he rented a room from his great uncle. Cheap accommodation would allow him to pay off his student loan in five years. The old man had stipulated that Darcy mind his own business.

He strolled down the corridor to the nurses' station. "Hello there." He smiled at the pretty blond in a snug uniform. "I'm the one who brought in Callum Bannerman, heart attack. How's he doing?"

An older nurse who was flipping through charts said, "Who are you?"

"I'm his nephew. I live with him at the farm. I should phone my mother." Darcy's voice trailed off. "Here's the thing: there's chores. I need to speak to my uncle as soon as he's awake."

"Okay. Write your name and phone number here." The nurse handed him a sticky note. "I'll let you know when he's out of ICU, probably tomorrow."

When Darcy arrived back at the farm about nine o'clock that evening, the German shepherd greeted him as he emerged from the mudroom, wagging its tail, eyes beseeching him.

"Hungry? Where's your food?" The dog danced in circles, chasing his tail, then barked twice, ran to the kitchen, and grabbed his bowl. "Okay, I get it already. Where's the food?" The dog skittered across the pine floor to the pantry, lay down, and again barked twice. "You're smart, aren't you, boy? Well then, what's your name, eh?" The dog barked twice more. Darcy opened the pantry door and found a large bag of dog food. He scooped a cupful and placed it in the dish. The dog followed him to a mat in the corner where his water bowl stood empty. Then he sat, the end of his tail thumping the floor. "Here you go, boy. Dinner." Darcy filled the water bowl and sat down while the dog ate.

On the farm where Darcy was raised, his family had owned a series of dogs, one after the other, always a replacement when one became too old or sick to work. They used to bring the cows in from the fields at milking time. When they showed signs of arthritis or needed vet attention, Darcy's father would take them out and shoot them. Then there would be another dog. Even though Darcy begged for a dog of his own, the answer came back the same: "No useless pets allowed."

One day, when he was ten years old, Darcy found a stray dog as he walked up the driveway from the school bus. The dog was a yellow Lab that followed Darcy home and hung around the house for days. Darcy's father forbade him to feed the stray, but Darcy saved part of his own dinner each night for the dog. He named her Queenie. The two of them were inseparable for a week. Finally his father sat down with Darcy and examined Queenie. He ran his hands all over her. Darcy thought he was checking to see if the dog was sound, would be strong for work, but that's not what he was up to. He found a tattoo in Queenie's ear. Darcy's dream ended. Queenie was sent back to her rightful owners. Never again would Darcy give his heart to an animal.

He decided not to phone his mother just yet.

The night after Uncle Callum's heart attack, the German shepherd followed Darcy around the house. When Darcy sat in the living room to read a magazine, the dog flopped on the rug beside his feet and snoozed. When Darcy went upstairs to bed, the dog went upstairs too. When Darcy shut the bedroom door in the dog's face, the dog set to whining until Darcy opened the door and let him in. The dog lay on the rag rug beside the bed staring at Darcy with guilt written all over his face.

"Okay boy." Darcy laughed. "You can sleep there, but just 'til Uncle Callum comes home." The shepherd laid his head on his paws and thumped his tail, once.

In Uncle Callum's hospital room the following morning, Darcy stood by the bed examining the tubes and machines and IV pole until Uncle Callum opened his eyes. "So, what's your dog's name? I forgot."

The old man closed his eyes. "Duke," he croaked through the tube in his mouth.

"I fed him, being as you're now an absentee landlord. So, how often does he get fed? Once, twice a day?"

"Twice. Two-thirds of a cup."

"Done," said Darcy. "Anything else?"

The weepy blue eyes examined Darcy. "Check on your grandmother."

"The old dame with the Cadillac? I don't even know her." Darcy zipped up his jacket.

The old man sighed loudly, as if a load of weariness was leaking out of his body.

Darcy couldn't help himself then. "Sorry you're feeling rough," he said. "I'll be back tomorrow."

After work in the afternoon, Darcy drove down the lane past the farmhouse. His grandmother lived across the river in a large yellow-brick Victorian home with gingerbread decorating the expansive porch. Surrounding the yard, old lilac bushes spread themselves like overgrown caterpillars. Darcy walked across the footbridge to her house.

His mother had brought him here once when he was nine after his grandfather died. He had not returned. His mother was a bitter woman who wouldn't talk about what had come between herself and her mother so Darcy felt at a loss. He crossed the summer kitchen and knocked on the door twice before he heard movement inside.

The essence of a little old woman clad in a black dress with turquoise shawl, purple stockings, and lace-up shoes stood in the dim light. At first Darcy thought she was wearing a lace cap on her head, but on closer examination, he discovered a purple streak in her hair that stretched from her crown to her forehead and down over one side of her curls. Gold hoops dangled from her ears and gold chains looped around her neck.

"Hello, dear," she said with a smile that crinkled her whole face. "Come in and have some tea."

"I can't stay long," Darcy blurted. "I have to feed the dog. Your brother, Callum, had a heart attack yesterday."

"Oh my! Well then, you absolutely must come in. He's not dead yet, I presume. Take your shoes off while I make tea and then we'll get to know one another."

Darcy did as he was told. If the old dear was inclined to talk, maybe he'd get some information. "Shall I turn on a light?"

"Do you find it dark in here? I don't notice. I'm almost blind, so it doesn't bother me. I like the twilight, don't you? The golden hour."

Darcy created a fresh image of his blind grandmother aiming her Cadillac down the centre of the road.

While she busied herself in the kitchen, she prattled. "I've owned the place ever since my father died, but I haven't actually lived here much since I was a girl."

"What were you running away from?" Darcy said, making assumptions, as usual.

His grandmother glanced at the ceiling with a little smile. "I wasn't running away from, I was running to. Someone very special. My husband was an engineer who designed huge river dams. The more successful the dams, the more in demand was his work. So, we travelled." She poured the tea. "Milk? Sugar?"

He nodded. "What about Mom? Did she go with you?"

"My one regret. Our lifestyle was not conducive to raising a family." She added a lump of sugar, stirred, and sipped her tea. "Have a biscuit. I'd say I made them myself but they're unmistakeably from the bakery in town. Is unmistakeably a word?"

"It sounds like a word to me. I understand it." The two of them laughed. "Tell me about my mother. What was she like as a girl?"

A pause interrupted the conversation. Darcy knew not to push for an answer. Sometimes the best information comes after silence.

In a soft voice, just above a whisper, his grandmother confided: "Callum sort of adopted your mother. He looked after her while we were away so she could go to school." His grandmother sipped her tea and stared out the window. "He became very fond of her."

Late that night as he lay awake in bed with Duke on the mat beside him, Darcy worked at putting two and two together.

The next morning he decided to call home. "Mom, Uncle Callum's in the hospital."

"Oh. I see," she said. "How are you? You don't phone and let us know anything."

Darcy winced. Same old, same old, he thought. "Mom, you never told me Uncle Callum looked after you when—"

"Looked after, is that what you were told?" she barked. "I suppose you've been to see your grandmother."

"So? Why shouldn't I? How come you never talk about her? How come you never visit her? What's the big deal with you?"

"You shut your mouth. I'm your mother. You don't talk to me like that."

Darcy felt her finger poking at his chest. "Fine. Have it your way. Uncle Callum had a heart attack. Thought you'd want to know. And I'm just great. Just great." He pressed End on the phone.

As he was setting out Duke's breakfast, then his own, he couldn't decide if he should go back to his grandmother's first, or to the hospital. He doubted Uncle Callum would open up. Darcy had studied psychology at university as part of his preparation for journalism. He often wondered why his mother was so bitter.

He walked down the lane with Duke. "Stay, boy," he said, before stepping up into the summer kitchen. The shepherd lay down obediently on the lawn.

His grandmother opened the door. "I saw you coming. The coffee's on." This morning she was all decked out in a sari of vivid blues and greens. She swept her way into the kitchen, then back again with two mugs of steaming brew. "What's on your mind today?" she asked.

"Well," he hesitated. "All right, did you miss my mother when you were absent from home?"

His grandmother took a long swallow of coffee. "All the women I knew who lived abroad as we did left children behind in the care of relatives. That was our normal. We didn't think it unusual. We didn't know any different."

"But did you miss your little girl? On birthdays? At Christmas?"

His grandmother stood up abruptly. "Why do you want to talk about all this? It's past. We can't go back. Would you like to see my photograph albums? I thought, being a journalist, you'd be interested in my travels." She swished past him toward a very tall bookcase.

Darcy stood up as well. "Of course. For sure. Maybe another time. Right now I have to run into the office."

He made his escape. As he walked Duke back to the farmhouse, he pondered his mother's history. Was she bitter because she had been dumped like an orphan? Was her marriage unhappy? Certainly his father was no prize as a breadwinner. Why was she so resentful toward Uncle Callum if he helped to raise her? As a boy, Darcy never questioned his family dynamics, but now he was curious. He wanted to know more.

His next stop was the hospital. Uncle Callum lay as still and grey as a corpse. Darcy watched him for a few moments until the old man opened his eyes. "How are you?" Darcy asked.

"Not dead yet," the old man said with a sardonic smirk.

"What is it about you Bannermans? So dark." Darcy moved the chair beside the bed so he could face his great-uncle. "I want to know what my mother was like as a little girl."

Uncle Callum reacted by poking at the air, the temperature gauge waving on the tip of his finger. "Trouble. Always trouble."

"Really? How so?" Darcy leaned forward as if he were about to receive a medal around his neck.

Uncle Callum suddenly became very agitated, rolling and thrashing on the bed. A nurse appeared in the doorway and hurried toward the machines attached to him. "You'll have to go," she snapped.

When Darcy settled down to work at his desk in the newspaper office, he typed *Bannerman* into the search engine. Dozens of articles popped onto the screen, mostly agricultural items, a few funeral announcements, then: "Bannerman boy found in river." Darcy scanned the news of a five-year-old boy named Charles who disappeared one March Saturday when the ice was breaking up. He printed the story and left the office.

He drove slowly back to the farm and down the lane. His grandmother opened the door. "Who was Charles?" he asked. "Was he Uncle Callum's boy?" His grandmother remained silent. "I didn't know Uncle Callum ever married."

"You're wrong," she said. "You'd better come in." She still wore her sari, but now it drooped on her like an old rag, her shoulders rounded under the silk.

Darcy felt suddenly afraid of what he was about to learn. They sat at the table.

"Charles was my little boy," his grandmother started. "He was three years younger than your mother. Such a darling, with golden curls, the sweetest child. He absolutely loved playing in water. He knew he shouldn't go near the river. Your mother watched over him to make sure. But he was a boy and determined. They wore snowsuits that day, so when he fell in…" She shrugged. "Well, you see what must have happened. Your mother didn't speak for weeks. Callum was destroyed—totally fell apart. He was guardian for both of them. Afterward, he wouldn't let your mother out of his sight. Everyone turned against me and your grandfather for not being here. Do you think if I had been home, I could have saved Charles?"

Darcy sat stunned. He could read the desperate sadness in his grandmother's blue eyes. He looked around the room at the photographs lining the walls, none of Charles. "You can't think like that, Gran. May I call you Gran?"

His grandmother laid her hand over his. "I don't think your mother ever recovered. Callum blamed himself too. Neither of them was the same again. As if a cloud moved into the house." Gran's face changed into an old woman's mask. Her purple hair streak appeared sadly ridiculous. "Actually, I hate it here," she said, sweeping her arm in an arc. "I think I'll go away. Somewhere exotic."

Darcy swivelled back and forth in his seat. "Why don't you tell me about your travels," he suggested.

"Agh," she muttered. "There's nothing in those albums that *National Geographic* can't tell better."

Darcy stood and moved around the table. He circled his arms around the old lady. "Don't go," he said. "I've just found you. Don't go."

When Darcy returned to the farmhouse, he phoned home. "Mom," he said. "Bake a pie. I'd like to come home on the weekend."

"Oh, just listen to yourself! This isn't a hotel, you know." She laughed.

Then he went to the hospital.

Richard M. Grove

EARLY MORNING NORTH OF MADAWASKA

On a silver-sliver-moon morning
I dipped my paddle
into the loon-echoed mist
of Victoria Lake.
Paddling toward waking island,
heavy underbelly of low-slung grey   drags
through black spires,   tree tips pointing
to Venus,   brilliant but fading.
Skimming ebony depths
kayak scrapes to rest
on red sandy shore.
Moments later long-shadow skinny-dip
zings me to life.
Breeze-cradled glide, unpaddled
sails me back as golden morning rises,
others now stirring.

Richard M. Grove

SKY GLIDING

Grey roots clutch
yellow clay bank
ready to slide
any moment
a century from now
over granite-boulder-strewn shore
into silent
breeze-rippled Victoria Lake.
Loons dip and dive
to chilled dark depths
corking to surface
wardling a warning
shy of sky gliding
kayak approach.

Donna Wootton

THE RED CANOE

In the morning Liz woke to find the air inside the cottage so hot and heavy it was hard to breathe. A dull light came through the slatted shutters, allowing her to see around a room made familiar by regular visits to their friends, Ray and Glenda. Her husband, Dave, was still sound asleep as Liz got out of bed and dressed as quietly as a mouse.

Finding Ray in the kitchen making breakfast she asked if he wanted her help but he declined. Free of obligation, Liz escaped outside. There, the air too was hot and heavy, but at least it was fresh. She inhaled deeply, sucking the summer ions into her lungs. Across the lake she could see morning clouds denting the sky above the landscape, the remains of the rising dew. It was calm, the lake surface flat, the shrill sound of a lone gull breaking the silence. She stood still for a long while. From her vantage point on the stone patio she surveyed the shoreline, where boats tied to docks bobbed gently. Most were covered with form-fitting tops that snapped into place to keep out the rain. The stillness overwhelmed her, pushing her to the verge of tears. Why tears? Why so emotional? She needed to move. Clear the mind. Stepping off the patio she headed down to the dock. Liz knew she wanted to be alone. She was imagining quiet, stillness, solitude, but before she could reach the dock, Dave stuck his head out the cottage door and called to her asking if she wanted to eat breakfast outside, and, of course, she said she did.

When she reached the patio Dave gestured broadly like an upscale inn keeper, a ghost of a grin on his face, inviting her to sit. It had been a dark night. Liz knew he was worried about her. Although they were physically close, she was emotionally distant.

The table outside was set with cutlery and condiments. Taking a chair Liz placed it behind the table so she could face the lake. Immediately Dave was at her side with a plate of eggs and toast.

Realizing she was being wooed, Liz thanked him. He told her not to wait for him, but to eat while everything was still hot, as if that was to her advantage.

When he returned Dave said Ray was with Glenda and they were talking in their bedroom so he didn't want to disturb them.

They ate in respectful silence before Dave asked what she was going to do after breakfast.

"It's calm on the lake. I was thinking I should go out in the canoe."

Dave looked over at the red canoe that he had strapped on the roof of their car. "I'll get it down for you." Then he looked at her curiously. "Are you saying you want to go alone?"

"Yes." Usually Dave sat in the stern and she paddled in the bow. "It's good exercise. Develop my muscles." Liz raised her arms and flexed her biceps. "Warrior Woman."

Dave stood and went to the car. He unhooked the roof straps. The red canoe was made of a layered polyethylene material that was indestructible. He could throw it to the ground if he needed to, it was that strong. Now he slid it off the roof and carefully supported it on his shoulders before turning it over and putting it down on the ground. From the trunk Liz retrieved the paddles and some gear and followed Dave as he dragged the canoe by the bow to the shore.

"Thanks, Dave. Hope you don't mind me deserting you?"

"If you don't mind if I read?"

"Not at all." Liz wondered if she and Dave were coping well with their new role of being empty nesters. The two of them were doing more together, finding common interests like the book club, but if she wasn't careful his constant presence could erase her. It wasn't as if they had grandchildren like Ray and Glenda to keep them busy.

"I'll help you with getting the canoe into the water."

Smiling at Dave, she thought it would be polite to accept his help. They slid the red canoe into the lake and moved it along the side of the dock. Dave held it while Liz scrambled into the middle by holding the wooden thwart. Fortunately the hull was shallow and flat. He handed her a waterproof cushion and she knelt on it to keep her centre of gravity low. Then she helped Dave strap the extra paddle along the ribs in the hull. She took the life jacket Dave offered her and put it on, tightening the side straps to fit snugly. No point taking any risks when on the water by herself. On her head she wore a wide-brimmed Tilly hat to keep the sun off her scalp. She picked up the single paddle, hers, which Dave had given her when they first started paddling. She thought it was a handsome paddle, made of cedar, a strong, light wood. The shaft and blade were polished. Grasping the shaft with one hand and gripping the butt with her other hand she set off.

On the water Liz stayed close to shore. Her sunglasses gave the world a tinted glow. The separated light particles sparkled over the surface of the water as if skipping to the tune of "The Bumblebee's Dance." Most of the other cottagers were bestirring themselves. Somewhere a screen door slammed shut; a baby cried; a vehicle drove along the gravel road; a man walked to the end of his dock and waved. Liz lifted her arm and returned his wave, then put both hands back on the paddle and laid it across the canoe. From her lake perspective the shoreline looked messy, a dirty contrast to the pristine water. She could look over the edge of the canoe and see minnows swimming on the bottom. When she lifted her head Liz saw a heron land on the shore. It stood erect and still. Waiting. Watching. Liz drifted. She too was waiting and watching. After a moment of reverie she again picked up the paddle and dipped the tip of the blade into the lake. Her enthusiasm for this solo adventure increased with every stroke.

Ahead was Betty Murphy's cottage. Drawing the paddle, Liz slowly steered the canoe past the cottage that remained intact after last year's storm though surrounded by destruction and death.

Betty called hello and motioned her over. Liz turned the canoe to shore and Betty walked down to the dock. She crouched and held the gunwale against the dock as Liz threw her the rope to tether.

While Liz waited for Betty to complete her task she raised her eyes and surveyed the property before asking, "Are those logs from the fallen trees?"

"Yes," Betty said. "What's left from the storm. I've lost my natural air conditioning. I hate not having any shade. Come inside."

Liz declined, saying she was out for a paddle but maybe another time. She felt protective of her time alone and maybe she appeared selfish but she knew what she wanted. She noticed a patch of daisies at the edge of the grass.

Betty said her granddaughters had picked some yesterday. "They're still asleep."

Relieved, Liz told herself that Betty had company. She didn't need hers. A morning breeze was now stirring the air. "Well, I'd better get going before the wind comes up."

Then the screen door slammed. The two women turned to see two girls, sleepy-eyed, both with bed-head, come outside. "Good morning," Betty called.

"Good morning, Grandma," they chimed.

"Sleep well? Want some breakfast?"

They plopped themselves into a low-slung chaise lounge, two thin bodies taking up the space of one large adult. "We had cereal." They looked so innocent, like babes in the woods, yet they were competent and independent enough to see to feeding themselves.

"Good for you, girls. Want to meet my friend, Liz?"

"Hi, Liz," they said in unison.

"The youngest is Selena and her older sister is Sarah," Betty said to Liz. Then she told her granddaughters that Liz had been one of the members of the rescue party after the big storm last year.

"Is she the one who knew your old boyfriend?" Sarah asked. "The man who died under the fallen tree in the driveway?"

"Yes. How did you guess?"

Liz did not mention that he was the only fatality of that terrible storm. It could have been so much worse.

When Betty resumed her conversation with Liz, Sarah turned to her sister, covering her mouth to talk, telling secrets. What did they share? Liz wondered. Aloud she said, "This is exactly the kind of day it was last year when the storm struck." Instinctively she looked up to see if there were any ominous clouds forming. Last year their appearance had been the first warning: dark clouds filling the sky before the wind started howling.

"It is," Betty said following her gaze. Standing she said, "Sorry, I'll let you get going." She untied the painter that tethered the canoe and waited while Liz back-paddled and then waved.

Liz was happy to be leaving yet her heart was not light. Betty, like Ray and Glenda, had grandchildren for company. Concentrating on pulling with all her might Liz thought about the display of photos on the fridge that Ray and Glenda had posted in full view for everyone entering their cottage to appreciate. Soon her arms ached with the effort of paddling, which brought her back to the task at hand. This red canoe was designed for river travel but was easy to handle on a large body of still water. It was small and sleek. It certainly wasn't as large as the ones the voyageurs had used when they transported furs in the north for The Hudson's Bay Company. Liz pictured those great vessels, which were thirty to forty feet long and held a dozen men and a heavy cargo that the men sometimes had to portage over rapids. Earlier explorers paddled on rivers, lakes, bays, crossing this vast land. How strong they must have been. Many of them worked until they were her age and older. How weak she felt by comparison. Dave had been her strong helmsman during all their water travel. She had to give him credit for being the one who first took her on outdoor adventures in a canoe. Although no voyageur, he was her partner and had introduced her to the great Canadian wilderness, places where no cottages were built along the shoreline, places that were still only inhabited by wild animals, places that were ancient. Those experiences counted for something. Those were memories they shared. Would they one day get to share them with grandchildren? Would there still be a wilderness for them to explore? Would the wilderness outlast all of them?

Liz looked across the water that was now shining like a crystal. She found she had drifted into the middle of the lake, where she did not feel comfortable being on her own. Carefully she dipped the blade into the water and turned the canoe back to shore.

On her return Liz paddled against a stiff wind. The land mass was stable but Liz was so focused on paddling she was past the dock before she realized she should turn into the cottage.

Liz was pleased that Dave was there to help pull the canoe out of the water. It seemed to her that he was offering her a rope. She had only one rope now to tether her. The small canoe felt heavy, heavier now than when she'd left: not just water-logged, but burdened by her reveries. The effort of taking the canoe out had been a challenge and she was fatigued. Now, beneath her feet the earth felt solid and steady. Her quiet solitude was gone, left behind when she'd paddled away on her own, but here was Dave ready to welcome her return to life on land. She smiled at him.

Peggy Dymond Leavey

INVISIBLE INJURIES

My father never talks to me about his wartime experiences. I'm too young to remember his coming home from Europe in 1943, and I certainly don't remember his leaving two years earlier. It was only last year, when I happened upon a newspaper article in one of Esme Tipple's scrapbooks, that I learned the full story of the battle that had cost him his right leg.

Esme Tipple is the aunt of my friend Sam, and a second mother to me. The Tipple family and ours are the only year-round residents of Lauder Lake, Ontario—winter population: six. Our families have known each other since before Sam and I were born, thirteen years ago last spring.

Esme lives in a silver Airstream trailer on the Tipple family property. She moved out of the big farmhouse she'd shared with Sam and his parents when she got engaged to Frank Fiske, a lineman for the phone company. Esme chose not to move back to the family home after Frank was killed in a car crash three years ago. She still hasn't built the house she and Frank had planned.

For as long as I can remember, Esme Tipple has been a "hello girl," one of the operators at the telephone exchange in Dexter Mills. She answers when you call Central, and then she plugs in the switch for the number you want. She was my mother's dearest friend from the time they were girls growing up in Lauder Lake.

The day I found the clipping with my dad's name in the headline, I had been scouring Esme's scrapbooks for pictures to illustrate my school assignment on the coronation. Esme has been saving pictures and articles for years and had already filled six scrapbooks. We sat at the table in her trailer turning pages crackly with dried paste, looking for any photographs of the royal family, beginning with the two little princesses and then the wedding of Princess Elizabeth and Prince Phillip and the births of their children, Charles and Anne.

"Sure, you can cut out that one," Esme agreed. "Just let me see what's on the other side."

While I waited I flipped open another scrapbook. Suddenly my dad's name leapt from a headline. I drew the book in closer. The article, written by a war correspondent, was dated December 26, 1943. "What's this? My dad was in the *Toronto Daily Star*?"

Esme craned to see. "And the *Dexter Detail* reprinted the story. Your dad was one of the local boys; people around here were anxious for any news from over there."

The war had ended for my father at the Battle of Ortona in Italy in December 1943. But until I read that newspaper article, I had no idea what my father had endured, nor what he and the other Canadian soldiers, after liberating towns all the way up Italy's Adriatic coast, had been up against when they reached the seaport city of Ortona.

It hadn't taken long for the Canadians to discover they had walked into a deadly trap.

The enemy was waiting for them, holed up in the houses that lined the main street. By first blowing up buildings and using the rubble to barricade all the side streets, they had left our soldiers no means of escape. As the Canadians advanced along the main thoroughfare, the enemy opened fire on them from the upstairs windows. Dad had been so badly injured by a land mine hidden in the debris that his leg had to be amputated. My mother must have known the story, but I had never heard it.

My dad and my grandmother and I live in the house attached to Moffat's General Store, the only store in Lauder Lake. It sits at the place where the lake road meets the paved road to the town of

Dexter Mills. The store used to belong to Gran, my mom's mother, but Dad bought it from her with the money he got from the government for being in the war.

Gran told me that she had hoped to buy her own little house in town when Dad took over, to move away from the store and Lauder Lake. She'd even started gathering cardboard boxes and packing some of her china. But then my mother got sick.

The summer I turned six, my mom started having bad headaches. The doctor in Dexter Mills sent her to the hospital in Peterborough. Except for one afternoon when she came to her hospital window and waved at me standing down in the parking lot, I never saw my mother again. She had a brain tumour and died in less than a week. Gran unpacked her boxes.

"Your dad has put the war behind him," Gran explained that day when I questioned her about what I'd just read at Esme's and asked why no one ever talked about it. Gran told me that after my father was wounded at Ortona he was in the hospital for a long time, first in England and then in Toronto. She said that my mother used to take the train down to visit him whenever she could.

According to Gran, our family was one of the lucky ones. My father had survived the war with his mind intact; others were not so fortunate. "Shell shock" and "battle fatigue" were terms she used.

Once in a while Dad's old wartime buddy, "Hughie" Harmon, would drop by the store for a visit. The Harmons lived in Dexter Mills, and their daughter Grace is a classmate of mine.

Our place is a long walk from town, and sometimes Grace's mother drops her husband off at the back door, although she never, ever, comes in herself. It's as if she's glad to be rid of Mr. Harmon for a couple hours. I know Grace is.

According to Gran, Mr. Harmon too had been wounded in the war. Once I asked, "What's wrong with him?" He didn't appear to be missing any limbs.

"Mr. Harmon's wounds aren't visible, Delia," Gran said.

Whenever we open the back door to Mr. Harmon, I see Gran's eyes dart to the parcel he holds tightly against his side. Eventually I figured out that Mr. Harmon's invisible injuries must have something to do with that brown paper bag he brings whenever he drops by.

On these occasions, Gran and I busy ourselves in the store, dusting shelves or straightening the tins of baked beans and boxes of laundry soap. We keep the door shut between ourselves and the men in the kitchen. "You would have to have seen what they saw, Delia," my grandmother explained once, over the sudden bursts of laughter that penetrated the wall. "You and I can never really understand what it was like. Over there." I just like the fact that Dad's friend can make him laugh.

My friendship with his daughter Grace is another thing, an on-again, off-again friendship, usually dependent on whether or not Sandra Parkhurst is in the vicinity. Sandra came to our school last year from a private school in Peterborough. She chooses her friends carefully and some people, like Grace, will do anything to be part of Sandra's elite group. If Sandra's around, Grace will start picking at me over the smallest thing, criticizing my clothes or my hair. By now I've learned to recognize the signs, and I just stay out of her way for a few days.

Earlier today I biked over to Grace's.

"I see you're still wearing that bathing suit," Grace remarked, watching me lift it from the basket on my bike. I hesitated long enough that she said, "Never mind. I'm glad you brought it."

"Well, you *did* say we were going swimming when you phoned this morning."

"I know, but we're not going to the community pool. Sandra called after I talked to you and asked me to come swim in her pool. When I told her you were coming into town, she said I could bring you too."

I hoped Grace hadn't begged to have me included. "You could've called me back. I wouldn't have cared."

"No, silly. You're coming with me. How many chances do you get to swim in a pool like the Parkhursts'?"

"Water's water." I shrugged. "I can always swim off Sam Tipple's dock."

"In the lake? It's freezing!"

Because Grace doesn't consider it chic to ride a bike, I left mine propped against her front porch, and we walked the six blocks to Parkhursts'. Sandra is the only person I know with a backyard swimming pool. Grace warned me ahead of time that it wasn't exactly kidney-shaped, like a movie star's, but it's gorgeous, just the same.

Sandra's father and uncle own a furniture store in Dexter Mills, as well as a funeral home out along the highway. "That's the reason the Parkhursts are so rich," Grace explained. "All funeral directors are rich."

Another thing the Parkhursts have is a television set in their rumpus room. I'd never seen a television set in anyone's house before, so as soon as Grace and I arrived that afternoon, Sandra led us down carpeted stairs to the basement.

Television is pretty new to Dexter Mills. Last Christmas, Gran and I stood in the snow on the sidewalk, part of a cluster of people watching a program through the plate glass window of Parkhurst's Furniture. Although the snow was thickening around us and my feet were freezing, I didn't want to leave. I couldn't imagine being able to watch the flickering black and white images in one's very own living room.

Now, in mid-July, we sat on the sofa in front of the television in Sandra's basement and waited for something to happen. Sandra turned the dial on the front of the set—thunk, thunk—as far as it would go one way and back again, but all we saw was what she called the "test pattern," a black-and-white picture of a North American Indian in full headdress.

"The shows don't really start till after supper," Sandra admitted.

I was practising my overhand crawl in the turquoise water of the pool, and Sandra and Grace were doing their best Esther Williams imitations on the deck above me, when suddenly Sandra's older sister and a half dozen of her high school friends burst through the gate, demanding we vacate the premises. We hadn't been in the pool more than ten minutes.

"Everyone out," Beverley Parkhurst ordered." This is my afternoon to use the pool, Sandra. And you know it."

Sandra hustled Grace and me into the garage where we waited, shivering, for Sandra to bring us the clothes we'd left in her bedroom. Five minutes later we let ourselves out a side gate onto the driveway.

"That was pretty rude," I remarked.

Grace shrugged. "That's just the way Beverley is."

"Then I'm glad I don't have an older sister, if that's the way they treat you."

"I guess you'd get used to it," said Grace. "Come on. Let's go to Gunter's and get a popsicle. I've got a dime so we can split one."

Sucking on grape popsicle we headed back toward Grace's. "You know what we could do sometime you come to town, Deeley? We could get a ride down to Bowes Lake with Beverley when she goes to work. Sandra's always asking me to go. There are some really cute boys working at the resort this summer, she says."

I tossed the stick from my half of the popsicle into the garbage receptacle on the street.

"And listen, Deeley. Sandra and I don't think you should spend so much time with Sam Tipple. Everyone thinks he's your boyfriend."

I bristled. Since when did Grace and Sandra get to discuss my private life? "He's more like a friend of the family," I said, then immediately hated myself for my betrayal.

To my relief, at that instant I spotted a familiar figure working in a yard up ahead. "Hey, Grace. There's your dad!"

Grace's father was on hands and knees, weeding one of the flower beds that lined the walk at the front of the community centre. "Hi, Mr. Harmon," I call out. He raised his head and, recognizing us, got to his feet.

"Why, hi there, Delia, Gracie. How's tricks?" He batted at the soil on the knees of his work pants. "Say, I'm just about finished for the day. If you wait a sec, I'll go get my lunch pail and walk back with you."

We were already halfway to the door when we realized we'd left Grace standing on the curb. "Unless you don't want to be seen with your old dad," Mr. Harmon teased, looking back at his daughter.

Grace rolled her eyes and dragged her feet to the door.

"I didn't know your dad worked here," I said in a low voice when she caught up.

"Big deal," Grace muttered. "He's just the janitor."

"Step inside, ladies," invited Mr. Harmon, "where it's cooler. I'll just be a jiffy."

The temperature in the spacious foyer was much more pleasant than out on the blistering pavement. Grace sank down onto a bench under the ticket window. "We can go if you want," she said. "You probably have to get back anyway."

"Ready to go, Satchmo?" Grace's dad reappeared. "Say, have you girls ever stopped to look at all these pictures on the patrons' wall here? Just take a gander. These folks were all big-time contributors to the campaign that raised the money to build this place."

"Are you two coming or not?" Grace had opened the door and now she stomped down the sidewalk ahead of us.

I stayed at the Harmons' only long enough to throw my bathing suit and towel into the basket on my bike.

"See ya later, alligator," Mr. Harmon said, before following Grace through the screen door and into the house.

"After a while, crocodile," I responded.

I heard Grace's "Oh, Dad. For heaven's sake!"

In spite of his goofy sense of humour and his constant wisecracks, and the way his visits seemed to worry my grandmother, I like Mr. Harmon. With me, he's always cheerful and funny. I feel sorry that Grace is embarrassed by him. I can't imagine how that would feel. But maybe, if you lived with him, you knew too much about those invisible war wounds.

Now that I think back, there is one early memory that sticks in my mind. It is of the day all the returning soldiers paraded down the main street of Dexter Mills. The war was over; I would have been about four. Dad was out of the hospital and home with us.

I remember my mother and grandmother and the little wire-backed chairs they sat on outside Dickinson's, the shop in town that sold chocolates and nuts. My memory is accompanied by the aroma of roasting hazelnuts.

Like everyone else in the crowd, we were waiting for the train that would bring the troops to the station. Dad sat beside us in his wheelchair. I don't think he had his artificial leg then, because he wasn't going to be part of the parade. It was a cold day, so it must have been winter. My dad had a blanket tucked around his hips, and my mittened hands were stuffed into my rabbit fur muff.

When the train finally arrived and the soldiers leapt down onto the platform, we all forgot the cold. The men marched down the street, swinging their arms stiffly and wearing huge grins. Everyone along the parade route was either cheering or crying. I remember the noise. Some of the men threw their berets into the air, and their families, tired of waiting, pressed forward. Little kids were lifted up to ride on their fathers' shoulders.

All of a sudden, one of the soldiers spotted us and broke out of formation. He seized hold of Dad's wheelchair and propelled him through the crowd and into the parade, pushing him along with all the other brave men and women in uniform.

And there my memory ends. What happened next? It was only later that I learned that the soldier who came for my father was Hughie Harmon. Maybe Grace was somewhere in the crowd too; I didn't know her then. Maybe they were all there, Grace and Mrs. Harmon and Beverley, all sharing that happy day.

Today, the nut shop is gone. There's a radio repair shop in its place. Esme Tipple buys her Frank Sinatra records there, and Esme says they have a soundproof booth where you can listen to a record before you buy it.

Wally Keeler

ELEGY FOR MY MOTHER

Reta May Keeler (01/11/1912—01/24/2004)

In your beginning was the blood and the breath,
the sharp inhalation of the carnal chaos of life.
Born 6 lb. 6 oz. in the pubescence of a century
of unprecedented carnage and creativity,
the State marked the occasion with certificate 12-05-037696.

In the un-electric world,
devoid of devices of diversion,
you flourished in family
and began your career
pushing placenta and parenthood
onto the open palm of life.

And so you earned
your Bachelor of Mom,
graduating into grandchildren
for the Masters of Mom,
but the world wasn't finished
with your dissertation of lineage
and great-grandchildren won you
the Doctorate of Motherhood

My trees are not yet barren
because it is September,
but for you, my mother,

a cold wind swept down
with January ferocity,
liberating your soul
for post-graduate work with the angels.

Your spirit is a kite tethered with umbilical love
and gentle unto the good days,
memories like random breezes tug
— what is the wind but a woman
loving us with caressing directions.

Your life straddled two millennia.
Your children born in peacetime
bracketed the world's worst war;
so I enjoyed your memories
of the pre-tech world,
of the pre-penicillin world;
from pre-flight to post-lunar landings,
your life was grounded
graceful as a backyard garden.

I regularly visited to mine your memories,
plucking nuggets of ageless gossip.

On the weekend of your death
I meant to ask you about your first kiss
but you replied with your last three diminishing breaths,
like the ellipsis ending of a love long life sentence…

WINNER OF THE FESTIVAL PROSE CONTEST

Hope Bergeron

THE GIFT

We buried the first of us in June. It had been a rainy spring but we were given a breezy, sun-splashed day for the funeral.

Time passed, slipping like sand through our fingers. We'd buried our grandparents and parents in turn. With disbelief, it was now one of us: The Kids.

Originally nine kids forever young we were: my sister, Diane the oldest; our cousins, Ric, Glenna and Brent before me. I was followed by cousins Deb and Bruce. Finally, baby brothers Paul and David arrived. A gaggle of brothers, sisters and cousins spanning eleven years.

Collectively, we now averaged sixty years of age. Where had the years gone, we "all for one" wondered?

Bound by childhood loyalty we escorted Brent to rest.

Nicknamed *hippie*. Remember? His brown curls tumbled to his shoulders. "Back in the day" that was the style. Remember?

We were from Toronto but thrived on the south shore of Rice Lake. Our parents built cottages from scratch. During the decades either side of centennial year, 1967, from Easter to Thanksgiving, we lived for The Lake.

We zombied through dull Toronto winters until the glorious free-range run of summer. Remember? "A place to stand…" We were in a funeral home, still standing together.

What a bitch piece of land our parents bought! Rocks, scrub, cedar, more rocks. It pitched straight down from the dirt road to the water. Who'd want this scrabble? Us. It became our reason to be, not knowing impossible. We willingly lost our hearts.

Our elders were tradesmen from lumbering; we kids, journeymen ready for adventure. Bucksaw, chainsaw, bonfire: we cleared our pitch.

We moved rocks and more rocks. Chain-block, block'n tackle or come-along: we pulled stumps and big rocks. What's a moraine? We all cussed rocks.

Foundations established, the back cottage walls hit The Hill, the front walls supported by pillars. Trusses, beams, shingles, stucco: our elders moved past the Depression, past the War, into the Space Age. We kids fell in with can-do attitude.

At the funeral, we were ignited by memories, still kids at heart. Remember taking building supplies up on the truck? No room in the cab, we rode the 401 in the truck bed with the stuff. "Sit down. Behave," Dad ordered. "If you fall out I can make another kid."

Knotty pine, mismatched lino tiles, second-hand furniture;

Beans 'n wieners,

French fries, hotdogs,

Peanut butter, white bread…

Grandma's brown sugar fudge—call The Kids to lick the pot.

We stacked firewood and fetched tools. We made cement, learning the difference between too wet or too short.

The Hill was terraced into gardens, rocks corralled into retaining walls. The year 1967 blazed a stylized maple leaf logo celebrating Canada's centennial. Dad cut a stamp out of wood proudly, permanently impressing the symbol into the wet cement of multiple sidewalks.

Grandpa painted the logos "Barbara Green." Then painted fence rails. Then porch chairs. Then (happily) ran out of this "free" paint he got from work. Grandpa'd give you the coins in his pocket if you could correctly guess "How much?" Never.

Other relatives came, more cottage kids, farm kids. The work, the play, the people reeled together like a fiddler's jig.

All Kids were good for a game—baseball in the gravel pit, badminton or bikes. There was a punt, a motorboat and a cabin cruiser. It could go sixty for skiing!

Remember? Let's go. Where?

Everywhere!

Muskie Bay for a Mountain Dew.

Boat? Walk?

Let's cut through the forest.

We can go to the island later.

…Need gas…

Kids congregated at the roadside swings. We played Dinky cars in the dirt. Barbie might arrive wrapped in designer fashion scraps salvaged from the ragbag.

Remember when Barbie's head popped off? She rocked the season headless, her bouffanted cranium later found where it rolled down The Hill.

Brent ironed my Barbie clothes. How the boys teased him! In later years he'd laugh, "Remember I ironed your doll clothes?"

Definitely, and forever.

We didn't care which kid showed up. Walk to the mailbox? Sure. Farther to Roseneath? Maybe there's horses out.

Look! There's mail! Flag's up!

Afternoons we'd pile up on the floating dock, radio bopping oldies when they were first time around. We'd toss each other off the dock. Who could squeal the loudest?

Skorts,
Pedal-pushers and halter-tops
Bell-bottoms, smock-tops,
Pirate shorts, bathing suits.
Stoked on Kool-Aid, we padded on dusty bare feet.

No matter whose table you turned up at, you were fed. Eat, get back to the game…

Sticky cards,

Lawn darts,

Eternal Monopoly.

Let's bake!

Fry's Cocoa Chocolate Cake, our specialty for a birthday.

We swapped magazines: *Mad*, *Teen Beat*, comics.

Let's go! Where?

Berry picking—dust-covered, roadside chokecherries, raspberries.

Try the apple orchard.

Might be cows.

Soooo, let's go. It's okay.

Hey, look! Here they come!

Quick! Climb!

Treed again.

Bark! Bark! Bark!

Here comes Boots!

Always a dog: Boots, Star, Major, Ask'im…

Cows away. Scramble down; carry on.

And the Great Corn Roast—five dozen corn. Parental direction: gather every kid you can find.

We'd watch summer wind ripple fields of golden oats. We'd watch one thousand sunsets sink behind Grasshopper Island.

The Roseneath Fair was anticipated for pull taffy. We didn't know the fair marked another year closing behind us.

The older boys worked on the farms; the farm kids would then come to The Lake to swim and fish.

There were antics.

The little boys set the treehouse on fire. The big boys with Toronto cohorts concocted a convertible. It started out as a hardtop.

When they cut the roof off, the doors fell off. Just weld the doors on, pile in over the top.

Ric coasted Black Beauty, their Buick, into a ditch. Brothers Paul and David took the prize. They tried to drive our two-tone blue '55 Buick—at ages five and six.

We were returning to Toronto on a Sunday evening. Only Paul and Dave ready in the car. Me, Diane and parents were scattered making our goodbyes to Uncle's family.

The Buick moved over the edge of The Hill.

Forget Barbie's head—Paul and Dave were going down the bitch-pitch to The Lake through Uncle's cottage, laughing all the way!

Until—

The car hooked a mere three-foot wooden lamppost, front tires spinning midair.

We got the boys out. The car tottered above the (evacuated) cottage until a tow-truck came to restore our respiration.

We lived to tell, casualties were few. Dave was dragged face-first down The Hill. The tree Dad was chopping slued sideways to take out Dave. Dad could only grab Dave's ankle—haul away! Make another kid indeed.

Aunty slipped down The Hill, suffering a broken leg.

Bruce, badly stung in the face by bees, couldn't open his eyes.

I flew over bike handlebars, my satin shirt as scuffed as me.

My sister, an unlicensed driver, took out a garden in Roseneath.

Poor Deb suffered the loss of her new NOT hand-me-down coat. I threw up on it, riding in their car. "You shoulda rode in the fresh air of the truck bed," Deb still reminds me.

We flew the first Canadian flag. Sure, we were getting the flag designed with blue borders. Ma made one. We saluted as it went up the pole. Then down it came, replaced by our true flag the government decided upon.

We always flew the flag, in Toronto too. Dad was buried with his flag.

Black and white TV had limited programming. *Tommy Hunter, Hymn Sing, Red Fisher* encouraged us to play outside. CHEX-TV, Peterborough, chimes *Theme From a Summer Place* as their theme. Whenever I hear it I'm transported back instantly.

The night of the moon landing everyone along the road crammed in to watch Space Age history on our TV, the air blue with cigarette smoke. Ma took slide pictures of the TV screen with her camera. They came out good. No one thought we might buy a newspaper by the time the film was developed!

Uncle got a telephone. Who'd call us, we're almost all here? When the phone rang Deb would answer, "House of Laughs"...

It was. Remember? We threw the boat anchor on that floating piece of marsh? The anchor fell through. Off we floated down The Lake until we unsnagged—family waving bye-bye.

Remember when the boat battery ran out (again)? Shore up, walk back through the forest, get the oars, walk back to the boat—and row!

Remember when Dave stepped on glass at the beach? We just got here! Patch him up when we go back.

Remember Ric shot the boathouse? "I wanted to see if the bullets would penetrate the walls." Diane and Brent inside.

And Brent blatted on that trumpet like Herb Alpert. "I'm Tijuana Brent," he crowed.

We thrived and drifted in and out: college, marriages, work. Years on, Dad voiced the truth we knew growing up. Whatever challenges incurred, like rocks, we lived in the greatest country in the world.

"You've no complaint," Dad would say. "You live in the Promised Land."

Today The Hill throws up irises.

Derek Paul

SCAVENGER

Turkey vultures circling o'er my chair
As I relax to take the air and sun
Look upon my scanty flesh—near none—
Hopeful of pickings, ready to be there
Should I breathe my last, this sunny day.
They would be here so timely for a meal
My eyes and brain would be the first they'd steal
And for the rest, they'd take it come what may.
And yet I'm not prepared to feed a vulture,
Though it might do well to pick my brain.
There's surely something telling in our culture
(Without ill will to vultures and their train)
That makes me think, "What's eaten and who eats?
Vultures scavenge; I can savour treats!"

Eric E. Wright

BORDER CROSSING

Saleem Hussain groaned. His wife Rani grimaced in frustration. Ahead of them stretched a mile-long line of trucks and cars waiting to cross into the US at St. Stephen's, New Brunswick.

Saleem came to a stop behind a semi hauling shipping containers. Fifteen minutes later they'd moved scarcely a hundred yards. Saleem tapped the map he'd been studying. "If we don't get going we'll forfeit our reservation in Vermont."

Rani sighed. "Maybe we should cancel that motel; find some place in Maine, or even on this side of the border."

Saleem pointed to a nearby Tim Hortons. "You take my place in the driver's seat, I'm going to get us some coffee and find out about local motels."

In the Tim Hortons he gave his order, then asked the freckle-faced teenager behind the counter, "Is it always like this?

"Ever since 9/11."

"Any other crossing with less traffic?"

"Locals use the Little Bridge crossing about five miles north."

Saleem ran back to their battered Honda, where he traded places again with Rani and pulled out of the lineup.

"What are you doing?"

"Going to another crossing north of here. The guy in Tim Hortons said there is never a lineup there."

Ten minutes later they crossed a short two-lane bridge over the St. Croix River and paused beside what looked like a weathered bus shelter. A grey-haired man set down his novel, peered at them from his perch on a stool, glanced at their Canadian passports and with a smile waved them on. "Enjoy your stay in America."

A few miles after they'd rejoined the main road, Saleem heard a siren. Glancing in his rear-view mirror he noticed a police car with flashing lights coming up very fast behind them. "Must be some accident ahead," he said, slowing down and easing onto the shoulder.

Suddenly, a helicopter swooped in front of them. From a loud-hailer they heard, "Stop the car and come out with your hands in the air."

Behind them, the police car screeched to a stop and two officers got out wielding submachine guns.

***

Saleem stretched to try and relieve the tension that gripped him. He massaged his shoulder as he glanced around the windowless room. At least a decade must have elapsed since the walls had been painted a nauseous shade of yellow. Scars marred the table at which he sat. His nose wrinkled from the stink of urine and mould. Saleem gnawed on his lip and wondered if the chain of dread pressing his chest was of his own creation. Or had it been programmed into the very walls themselves?

The door opened. The same grizzled officer who had already interrogated him for an hour reappeared. He sat down opposite Saleem and stared silently at him for some time.

Saleem looked away and sighed deeply. Then he turned back to face the officer. "I've already asked you several times what this is about. I've asked for a lawyer. Please, get me a lawyer…I demand a lawyer?"

The grizzled officer smiled. "Demand, Mr. Hussain? You're not in a position to demand, but if you cooperate everything will be peachy." He reached up and smoothed his comb-over into place.

"Tell me again. Why did you cross at Little Bridge instead of St. Stephen's, New Brunswick—unless you've got something to hide?"

Saleem slumped in his chair. "I've told you a hundred times. St. Stephen's had a huge lineup. A local kid told me about Little Bridge."

The officer leaned forward and struck the table. Saleem recoiled.

"Ah yes, your local contact. Who is he?"

Saleem threw up his hands. "Not a contact. Some kid working at Tim Hortons."

The officer snorted. "Tim Hortons. That's rich."

"Look, I'm a Canadian citizen. You've seen my passport. You have no right to hold me or my wife."

"No right?" The officer waved his finger in Saleem's face. "No right? You're on our watch list." He waved a sheaf of papers. "Right here, S. Hussain."

"S. Hussain? Hussain is a common name. There are thousands of Hussains in the Toronto phone book."

"This report is from Homeland Security. We don't make mistakes. It says right here you're from Peshawar in Pakistan. You spent six months in a terrorist training camp. You travelled to Saudi Arabia for further training. And you've been biding your time in Canada for just the—"

Saleem jumped up. "No! Not Pakistan. India. I'm from Mumbai…"

***

On the third page of the January 5 edition of the *Moncton Herald* a short news item appeared. "Mr. Saleem Hussain, business manager of Ocean Fashions, and his wife Rani disappeared while travelling to Syracuse to celebrate Christmas with their son and daughter-in-law. The Moncton police are baffled by the case. They have found no clue as to their whereabouts."

Gwynn Scheltema

BABES IN THE WOOD

Cold burrows deep into her bones. Catches in her throat. Settles in her heart. From the eighth-floor apartment she looks for the forests and lakes reflecting blue brilliance of sky. Looks for the Canada of the brochures, of the postcards, of the paintings in the embassy. But everywhere bare-bone branches wail arms against the sky, stamp their feet in grey earth. This is not what she wanted to come to. Today's sky stretches thin blue like vein beneath skin.

Perhaps she left her capacity for joy on that airport runway on the other side of the world. Even now her body reverberates with the muddle of hope and sorrow she felt as the plane took off. She remembers the shivering, her teeth clattering in her mouth, her head stiffening against thought. "Ma'am? Are you all right? Can I get you water? A doctor? Are you ill?"

But she wasn't ill. Couldn't they see the spilling of tensions about her, discarded on the floor, slipping down the aisle? False accusations. Frantic phone calls. Armed escorts. And wakeful nights throwing things in suitcases. All being expunged; relief flooding through every pore to fill the vacuum. "No, I'm not ill. I'm safe."

She still guards her words in this new place, does not yet know whom to trust and with what. "Yes, the foreign transfer has come through," the bank teller offered just yesterday. "Do you want it in cash?"

"Shhh," she'd said out loud, looking to see who may have heard. Then the realization. "I'm sorry," she'd muttered, head down, voice low. "It's just that…. Never mind." A weak smile. Embarrassment. "You wouldn't understand."

These apartment windows open only at the top. These walls close in on her. She needs air. She's never lived in an apartment before. Never been on the eighth floor of anything. She wants to open her door and step into a garden, to smell jasmine and hear the call of the louries. She wants the warmth of the sun on her face. Far below just at the corner of the building she sees a scrap of green in a group of trees. A footpath leading in. It calls her.

She opens the apartment door and steps into the hallway. Turns to leave and remembers. Catches the door just before it closes, and returns inside. She grabs her coat and tries again.

When she steps out of the elevator a young woman her age is fussing with a toddler. She cannot tell if the child is a boy or a girl in the cocoon of clothes. The woman smiles at her. "Isn't it great? Spring's finally here," she says. "The creek's running something fierce. All the snow melt, eh?"

What to say? What is snow melt? She's never seen real snow. Only pictures in her childhood books from long ago. Mounds of white with sleighs and happy children and colourful scarves. Perfect round snowmen with black hats and carrot noses. But there is no snow outside. The woman looks straight at her, waiting for a response.

"Trees all budding now," the woman tries again, "and the sun is just glorious."

She can't find words to answer, so she pulls her coat tighter about her, makes for the lobby door. But outside, this northern sun doesn't feel "glorious." It's too weak, too cool. And the wind cuts like a whip. She glances around as she takes small steps down the sidewalk. People walk differently here. They watch where they step, heads down, necks turtled in sweaters. They walk with their eyes only, not with their ears and their noses. She knows the sound of a snake comes to you long before you see it on the path; the smell of stinging ants reaches you before you find their trail in the grass.

To be safe, you must walk in the world, not on it.

She passes the playground, where children creak the metal chains on swings and mothers chat at the fence, blow on their fingers. There is no fear in their eyes. One day she may be part of those conversations, but right now she doesn't fit here, and there is a greater need to be filled. She must find a place to feel the earth, to reconnect.

A few steps more and she reaches the edge of the trees. The footpath leads down into them and away out of sight. In the distance she can hear water running. The path calls to her, but every sense tells her not to proceed. The trees are thick here. They have no leaves, but old dead branches and knotted vines block out the light. She wonders if this is a forest or a wood or a copse or a thicket. She remembers these words from her books, but she doesn't know how they are different. She closes her eyes, tilts her head back and breathes. She struggles to remember the illustrations from those childhood fairy tales, the dark woods. They had tangled vines and dead branches too.

Dampness rises from the ground and assails her nose with the unmistakable smell of mud and frogs. At last, something is familiar. For a while she stands and lets it all soak in, but voices break into her thoughts.

"Sorry, can we just get by?"

She steps aside. Tucks her hands under her armpits. The young girls skip by, ponytails swinging, ears wired with earphones. She wants to shout, "No, don't go in there! It's not safe." But doesn't. Again the realization. The inner embarrassment. This is Canada.

Deliberately she tells herself: There are no landmines; there are no snakes. Be brave. If she can do this one thing, she can do anything. One step. Another. She moves down into the trees.

The heavy air chokes her. A few steps more and she cannot see the entrance. She presses her lips together, tastes cold sweat.

Breathes. Just breathes. Recalls the story of "Babes in the Wood" and understands their fear.

At her feet the curled beginnings of ferns poke through damp leaves rotted to lace. A sprig of green hope. She breathes again. And ahead more green carpets the rocks. She hurries to touch it. Hesitates at the coarse, wiry mass. Reaches out just one finger.

And beneath her touch she feels softness. Moss. This is what moss feels like. Soft, cushiony, welcoming. And she laughs out loud, feels muscles in her body relax one by one. The page to her childhood stories has opened and this time it makes sense. This is what those babes slept on; this was their forest bed. All these years she had thought what silly children to lie on the ground at night among the snakes and the ants. Why did they not climb the highest tree, pray that leopards were not close?

But now she knows. And she is not one of the babes in the wood. In this place the choices are different. She can leave old worries on that faraway airport runway and reclaim her capacity for joy.

She breaks off a small piece of moss, cradles it in her cupped hands. Back in the apartment she places it on damp tissue on a saucer in the window. Through the window the warm sun bathes her face. She smiles.

Kim Aubrey

FRAMES

From bedroom window, I watch a beach walker
flourish a long white pennant that trails behind him,
transforms into a wave, lays its white cloth to dry
on shore the same moment he vanishes
beyond frame, taking the magic with him.

An hour later I wait for a freight train to pass
so I can drive over tracks into the Via Rail lot,
catch a passenger train to the city. I can see
only the brief length of containers held
by the frame of personal periphery,

part of an endless magician's handkerchief,
parade of towels hung on a line—red, yellow,
blue of children's cereal boxes. Wonder
about the prize inside, anxious to know
when this show might end.

In Saskatoon we once waited twenty minutes
on an airport drive for a freight train to finish
unfurling, but did not miss our flight. And I don't
miss my ride to the city, but a bearded man
sleeps in my assigned place.

Awakened, he startles, struggles to find
phone, gather shoes, read his ticket.

I offer to take his seat, twin of mine
in the next car, but doors won't open.
Attendant has to pull push until they give.

Lately I seem to invite obstacles, as if my way
has been too easy. Maybe a reminder
that what feels hard could be much harder,
and the sleeping man might have arrived
from a place of unthinkable losses.

Settled in Car Three, my gears shift to grateful
for the vacant seat beside mine absent the fug
of someone else's sleep. The world does not owe
me a thing, has already given of its bounty,
enough magic to keep anyone going.

CONTRIBUTORS

Kim Aubrey's writing has appeared in *The New Quarterly*, *Numero Cinq*, *Event*, *Best Canadian Stories*, and others. Kim's story collection, *What We Hold in Our Hands*, was published in 2013. Kim was born in Bermuda, where she leads an annual writers' retreat. She lives in Cobourg.

Hope Bergeron retired after a career in visual arts: Stratford, Canada Trust, The Globe and Mail and Eatons. Surprisingly, time as a Loblaws cashier was just plain fun. Travels took Hope to Russia, Europe, the Arctic, Costa Rica and the US. Legally blind, Hope sits as volunteer vice-chair on the Northumberland Access for Disabled Advisory Panel. She encourages everyone to explore the adventures of talking books.

Christopher Black says he's just a traveller through time, a student of life, a lawyer, an actor, a poet, a guitarist, sharing some thoughts with fellow travellers, in poetry, in prose, in any which way they come to him.

Alan Bland is employed in the international insurance industry and also in writing opinions as a court expert witness on insurance matters in Ontario. He is a writer, photographer and cook who plays the saxophone. He moved to Northumberland five years ago, as an escapee from the GTA.

Jennifer Bogart, reader, writer, editor, explorer, dreamer, is having a love affair with words. Author of three women's fiction novels (*Remember Newvember*, *Reflections*, and *Money, Masks & Madness*), one serialized novel (*Sunny with a Twist of Olive*), and one YA fantasy series (*Liminal Lights* and *Shadow Shifts*), she can't stop writing any more than she can stop breathing.

Patricia Calder is the author of *Roadblock*, a novel about two boys recovering after the deaths of their siblings. Many of her articles and stories have been published since 1974. Her equine photography is well known throughout Northumberland County. She taught English, journalism and writing for thirty years in Ontario. patriciacalder.ca

Sharon Ramsay Curtis likens herself to a hand-made quilt, which grows from whatever materials are at hand. Her creative life has gained inspiration from the amazing people and experiences she has met with. Lately writing and illustrating stories has become a focus. She anticipates all kinds of excitement and learning ahead.

Bill Daniels has been writing for over forty years for newspapers, magazines, radio and now freelance. He wrote advertising copy for a large chain store, as well as radio commercials. He has published poetry in the *American Anthology of Poetry*, and published a book on women's self-defence. He is presently cleaning up a book of poetry and writing short stories.

Pegi Eyers is the author of the award-winning book *Ancient Spirit Rising: Reclaiming Your Roots & Restoring Earth Community*. She lives in the countryside on the outskirts of Nogojiwanong (Peterborough, Ontario) in Mississauga Anishnaabe territory, on a hilltop with views reaching for miles in all directions. stonecirclepress.com

Lori Felix is an artist living in Hastings. She loves to transform photos into original artworks. Using clients' vintage photographs and portraits, or home, car and pet photos, Lori creates custom artwork. Lori's portfolio and videos of the way she works can be seen on her Facebook page: Be a Part of the Art by Lori.

Kim Grove has been published in the *Globe and Mail, The Christian Science Monitor,* the *Toronto Star* and various smaller publications. She has taught writing at Loyalist College and the Trenton Air Force Base. Her teaching comes from a love of reading what others have to share.

Richard M Grove / Tai lives in Presqu'ile Provincial Park, halfway between Toronto and Kingston. He is the man of eight Ps—Poet, Publisher, Photographer, Painter, President, Public Speaker, Potter and Person. He runs HiddenBrookPress.com and is founding president of the CCLA—CanadaCubaLiteraryAlliance.org. His many book titles can be found on Amazon.

Marie-Lynn Hammond is a singer-songwriter, editor, writer and former CBC radio broadcaster. Co-founder of Stringband, one of Canada's seminal folk groups and indie-record pioneers, she's known for her intricate lyrics and her subject matter, which often incorporates Canadian themes. She's been happily living in Cobourg since 2015. marielynnhammond.com

Maggie Harper is a retired medical lab technologist with a love for words. She refers to her writing as vagabond prose. The daily ritual of haiku centres and promotes focus. This process has nurtured her respect for the discipline and work that writing requires. A novel lurks within.

Katie Hoogendam is an American transplant from a tiny little town near the shores of Lake Michigan. She lives and writes in a bigger little town on the (Canadian) shores of Lake Ontario.

Shane Joseph is a graduate of the Humber School for Writers and the author of four novels and three collections of short stories. His work *After the Flood* won the best fantasy novel award at Write Canada in 2010. His latest collection of short stories, *Crossing Limbo*, was released in 2017. shanejoseph.com

Wally Keeler is the founder (1973) and creative director of the Imagine Nation of the Peoples Republic of Poetry. Wally is a multi-media poet utilizing photography, film, video and computer data processing technology to create and document poetic events. Wally has been published in many of Canada's top literary/art zines.

Norma Keith, after relocating from Toronto to Rice Lake and finding an incredible canvas of nature's beauty, embraced her passion for photography. Her preference is for shooting rural landscapes and wildlife and creating monochromatic images. She has received many awards, and her work is available at exhibitions and on creative art cards.

Alan Langford has settled on the phrase "multimedia artist" as an umbrella for his many creative explorations. Primarily working in glass art, photography and digitally manipulated photography, he also occasionally writes, paints, draws and builds things.

Peggy Dymond Leavey, a former librarian, is the author of thirteen published books that include juvenile novels, local history and Canadian biographies of Mary Pickford, Laura Secord and Molly Brant. Her book, *Laura Secord, Heroine of the War of 1812*

(Dundurn Press), was a finalist for the Ontario Speaker's Book Award. Peggy lives in Quinte West. www.peggydymondleavey.com

Gerry Malloy is a former automotive engineer and long-time automotive journalist and editor. He is a three-time winner of the Canadian Automotive Journalist of the Year award as well as several other honours. He has lived in Northumberland County for thirteen years and is currently editor of Autofile.ca.

Linda Hutsell-Manning taught two years in a one-room school and completed a BA from Guelph University before beginning to write. She's the author of eleven published children's books; poetry and short fiction in literary mags; a novel, *That Summer in Franklin*, Second Story Press; a novella, *Heads I Win*, short-listed by Quattro Books; and a two-act comedy, *A Certain Singing Teacher*, which premiered with VOS Theatre Cobourg this year.

Maureen Mullally is an artist, singer and writer. She has lived in Northumberland County for over fifty years and enjoys everything it has to offer. She contributed to both *Hill Spirits* and *Hill Spirits II* and is pleased to have another story published in *Hill Spirits III*.

Reva Nelson is a professional speaker and writer who thinks one of her best decisions was to move to Cobourg. She leads workshops on presentation skills, memoir-writing and how to write and present eulogies (not to be morbid, but it's a good skill to have at a certain age). Reva enjoys reading, talking, petting other people's dogs and dark chocolate. revanelson77@gmail.com.

Derek Paul is a retired physicist who also became a peacemonger and a peace researcher and gradually a generalist. He has published papers or chapters in books in various fields. His current work is on ecological economics, which he believes must be the new way of conducting human economic affairs if civilization and indeed humanity is to survive.

Tom Pickering's writing career started as a developer of training manuals for engineering and technical companies. He wrote and directed original plays that were produced in community theatre. Currently, he is writing short stories and providing help for people to record their own life stories through yourstoriedlife.ca.

Marie Prins is a remedial reading teacher with her own practice, The Reading Room. She lives with her artist husband in an historic, octagonal home in Colborne. Over the past ten years, she has written memoir pieces, poetry and children's stories. She has completed writing a children's novel and is seeking a publisher. Most of her work, which can be found at marieprins.ca, is inspired by the history of her home and its surrounding gardens.

Felicity Sidnell Reid writes poetry, short fiction and non-fiction, some of which has been published in anthologies and online journals. Her novel *Alone: A Winter in the Woods* was published in 2015. She is the co-host of the radio series *Word on the Hills* (Northumberland 89.7 FM). felicitysidnellreid.com

Cynthia Reyes has been blessed with a career as a creative leader and writer, and as a business leader of complex projects in Canada and internationally. A writer of literary non-fiction, her work has been published in the *Globe and Mail*, *Toronto Star*, *Toronto Life* and *Arabella Magazine*. With her books *A Good Home* (2013) and a further memoir *An Honest House* (2015), Cynthia now adds "author" to her career achievements.

James Ronson is a lifelong traveller, writer and educator. "Flood" is his third short story. His novel, *Power and Possessions*, was published in 2015. James is currently writing a work of historical fiction about the early days of hockey in Canada. He lives with his wife in Port Hope.

Erika Rummel divides her time between Ontario and Los Angeles. She is the author of four novels, *Playing Naomi, Head Games, The Inquisitor's Niece* and *The Effects of Isolation on the Brain*. Her most recent nonfiction book is *A Nobel Affair: The Correspondence between Alfred Nobel and Sofie Hess*. She tweets @historycracks and blogs at http://rummelsincrediblestories.blogspot.ca/.

Gwynn Scheltema was raised in Rhodesia, now Zimbabwe, and her writing is shaped by that remarkable and rich landscape. Arriving in Canada in 1982, she balanced her practical accounting background with a passion for writing. A poet, columnist, non-fiction writer, novelist and professional editor, Gwynn has won several awards for her writing including the Timothy Findlay Creative Writing prize. Gwynn is also producer and co-host for *Word on the Hills* radio show on Northumberland 89.7FM.. writescape.ca

René Schmidt wrote a series of books on Canadian disasters by Scholastic Canada, and his fiction novel *Leaving Fletchville* was a Red Maple Honour Book in 2010. He has published magazine articles and sold plays. René graduated from the Creative Writing program at York University. René lives near Trenton with his wife, Shirley.

Susan Statham is an artist and an author. She recently completed *The Nation Builders*: paintings of twelve of Canada's prime ministers. She is the author of *The Painter's Craft* and winner of the

Medli award (for best manuscript by a published author) for *True Image*. She is an editor of, and contributor to, the anthologies *Hill Spirits*, *Hill Spirits II* and *Hill Spirits III*. sstatham.com

Diane Taylor is the author of *The Gift of Memoir*—a guide book on memoir writing. She also wrote *From the Heart of the Ship*, a memoir about her life at sea. She has written dozens of articles for *Canadian Yachting*, *Cruising World*, *The Journal of Palliative Care*, and other magazines, and gives workshops in memoir writing.. dianemtaylor.com

Donna Wootton is pleased once again to have a poem and story included in this *Hill Spirits* anthology. She has written a new novel that will be published in 2018. dmwootton.com

Eric E. Wright's eclectic experiences include sixteen years in Pakistan followed by ministry in several pastorates and teaching stints in a Toronto seminary. Among his eleven published books are four suspense novels including his latest, *Rust Bucket.* He lives with his wife, Mary Helen, in Port Hope. countrywindow.ca

CPSIA information can be obtained
at www.ICGtesting.com
Printed in the USA
LVOW03s1003300917
550638LV00002B/2/P